Love, Abused

A Record of What Was Seen and Not Acted On

Author Note

This book draws on lived experience and on contemporaneous records held by statutory services. Where possible, the language of those records has been preserved. Names, locations and identifying details have been altered to protect privacy.

This is not a comprehensive history, nor an attempt to establish a definitive account of events. It does not seek to assign guilt or deliver judgement.

What it presents is a pattern, built from documentation, observation and memory, and from the space that exists between them. It records what was seen, what was missed and what endured.

The perspective of the child is necessarily partial. Much of what is described was not understood at the time, and some of it only later. The records do not resolve that gap. They sit alongside it.

I have resisted the impulse to interpret events beyond what can be shown. This includes resisting the language of recovery, redemption or closure. Where the book appears quiet, that quiet reflects the way harm presents when it is managed rather than addressed.

This is one account. It does not stand in for others, nor does it claim to speak universally.

The work ends where the paperwork ends. What follows exists outside the record.

For my Mum, Helena

Another day passes, another year, and with them comes another smile I put on to keep the room steady, to reassure the people around me that I am coping, at least well enough for now. It is a rehearsed emotion, one that no longer surprises me. I know how to wear it without thinking. It fits easily, even when it has nothing to do with what I feel.

The tears come less often. That much is true. But the ache has not softened or shifted with time. It sits where it always has, constant and familiar, a quiet weight carried forward rather than released. Loss does not always announce itself loudly. Sometimes it settles in and stays.

You gave up so much for a child who should never have had to survive what he did, and that knowledge still presses in on me. It lives alongside everything else, inseparable from who I am and how I move through the world. Love and damage are not opposites. They exist together, unresolved.

I still find myself waiting for your smile, the one that filled the room and made everything else feel calmer, lighter, briefly safe. My body remembers it before my mind catches up. My arms lift without thinking, reaching for a hug, and then fall again when I remember there is no one there to meet them.

The phone stays dark in my hand. No call. No message. Just a blank screen reflecting back the absence I already know too well. Silence has its own sound, and it grows louder when it is expected to break and never does.

Mother's Day approaches whether I am ready or not, marking time in a way that feels deliberate and unforgiving. It asks something of me that I cannot give. And in that space, there is only the steady weight of loving you and the quiet, enduring pain of not seeing you again.

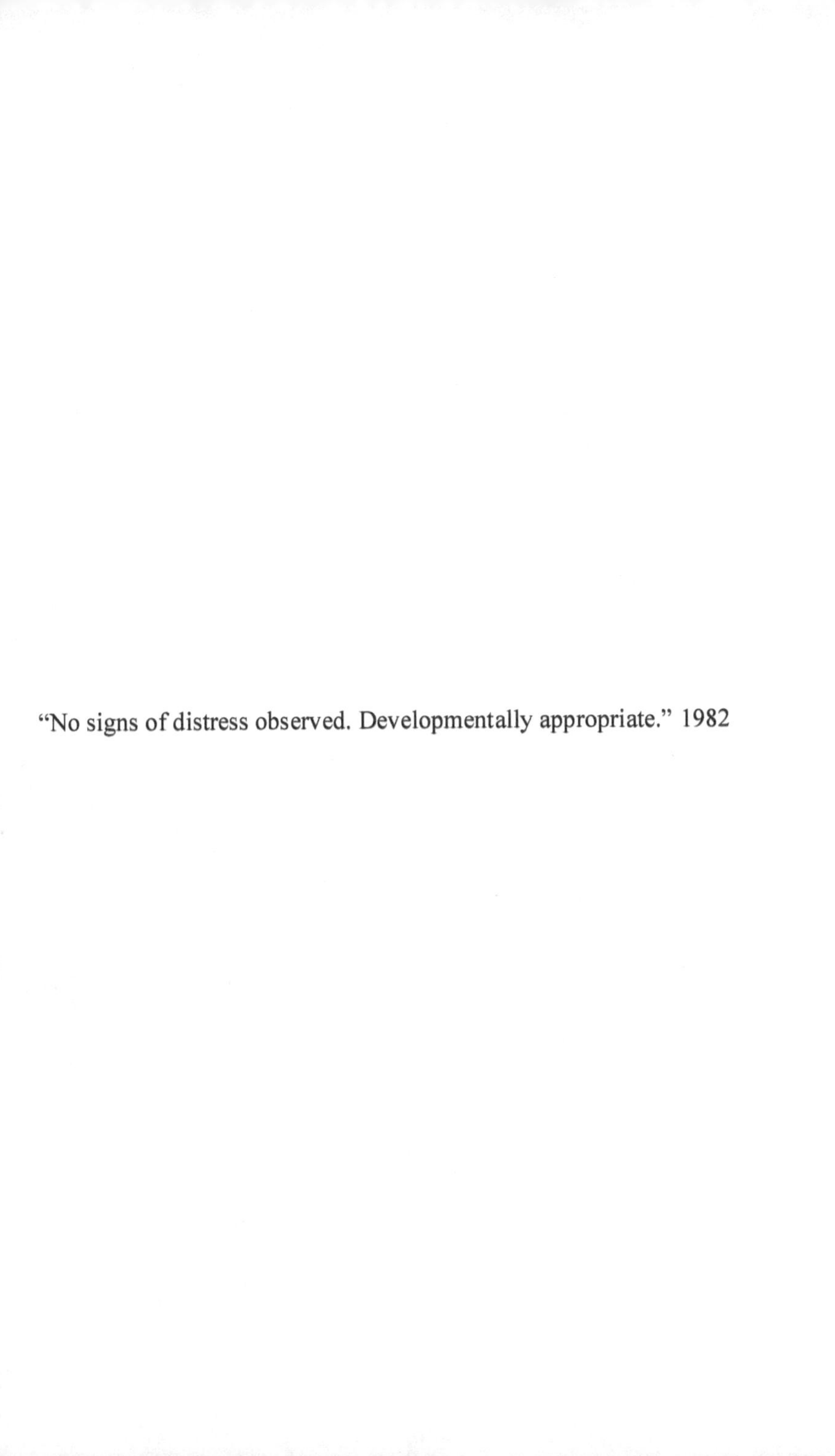

"No signs of distress observed. Developmentally appropriate." 1982

"He didn't speak that week. Not to me. Not to anyone. But he screamed in his sleep." 1984

This is a record. Not of what was hidden, but of what was seen and not acted on. What follows is drawn from notes, reports and memory, and from what the body kept when the file moved on.

Origin

Jemma's father is present early on in the document, most often accompanied by a figure denoting an incident number or a police reference, his name typed and abbreviated, reduced to labels that are repeated in varying forms. Aggressive. Volatile. Alcoholic. These words are explanation enough. There is no discussion of how often he drinks, what he is like in the hours preceding the shouting. There is no description of what a house sounds like when a man is angry, or how that anger can build for hours before anything at all happens. There is only discussion of outcome. Of attendance. Of involvement.

Inside this house, fear is a familiar state. It is not a state that descends in a rush of panic. It is a state that is present early and often. It is a state that informs routine, that alters the way people move from one space to another, that causes people to keep their voices low and their questions unasked. Jemma learns early on how to read her father's mood, how to sense the weight of his footsteps on the stairs, how to differentiate between silence that is calm and silence that is not. She learns this not by being told. She learns it by living.

Alcohol is always there, even when it is not causing trouble. The drinks seem to appear on the table, in the bin, next to the sink. The drinking is so much a part of the evenings and weekends that it is hard to imagine anything else. He is kind when he is sober. These things complicate everything. They complicate it so much that it is hard to put your finger on just what is wrong. They complicate it so much that it is hard to be hopeful that things will stay this way, as long as everyone behaves, as long as no one makes demands, as long as no one makes trouble.

Violence is not constant. That makes it hard to predict, hard to explain. The violence comes and goes. There are apologies, promises, and then peace. It is as though it has all been earned. Jemma quickly realises that staying is good, leaving is bad. Leaving makes trouble. Pointing out what is happening behind closed doors makes trouble. Jemma quickly learns to manage her reactions, to manage her expressions, to manage her body. These are things she will be praised for in the future, for being strong. When police come, it is usually late in the evening. The flashing lights come and go quickly. The voices drop in volume. The adults talk. Jemma stays in another room, sits on the stairs. She listens. They are polite. They have questions, write things down. They leave. The house immediately goes back to normal. The record is kept. Attendance. No further action. The words appear several times. They neatly tie everything together, even though nothing has really changed.

Her father's anger is a physical presence. It occupies space. It determines who talks and who does not. Jemma discovers that the men around her control the environment. Their emotions define the mood. Everyone else reacts to them. This is a lesson that Jemma absorbs. It is a lesson that influences her perceptions of relationships. It is a lesson that influences her perceptions of love. Love is something that can shift quickly. Love is something that is dependent on others. Love is something that is fleeting.

Love in the home was unpredictable. Some actions indicated a level of care, actions that complicated the situation. A hand up in the lift, money changing hands, a joke told in good times. These are facts, and they are important. They make it more difficult for Jemma to have a clear idea of what was happening to her. They make her situation confusing rather than comfortable. She learns to expect the inconsistent as normal, to work hard in good times in the hope that they will continue.

The recording focuses on the father in the background. He is context, his actions providing background to Jemma's situation. Her situation is complicated by his actions, but they are not directly addressed. Domestic abuse is mentioned as a complication, but not as a direct action. It is relegated to the margins in all reports, important but not important enough to act on. The focus remains on Jemma, her actions, her reactions. The adult in power fades into the background.

Jemma assumes adult roles at home early on. She learns to read needs, to ensure things run smoothly where possible. She learns to avoid conflict through compliance, through speed, through staying out of the way. This becomes second nature to her. She takes it with her wherever she goes. It is misinterpreted by adults as independence, as maturity.

There are moments when the fear is intensified, when the violence escalates, when objects are thrown or voices are raised to a pitch that makes the air feel thin. Such moments are recalled vividly, if not talked about. Jemma does not need to recall such moments consciously. Her body recalls them. She remembers the knowledge of how quickly things can change, how little warning there is, how unsafe her home becomes without warning.

When professionals talk to Jemma about her father, the questions are simple and circumspect. Is everything OK at home? Do you feel safe? The questions are asked in places not safe enough to answer truthfully. Jemma provides the answers to keep things moving. She knows that if she provides too much information, the consequences are beyond her control. She knows that the truth does not necessarily set one free. She knows this later. She knows it as evasiveness.

Jemma's father's drinking is talked about as a problem, but it is talked about as his problem, not as a problem for others. Solutions are suggested. Solutions are offered. He might go to meetings, might promise to cut down. Such actions are seen as positive. The question is soon asked if Jemma is managing, if she is going to school, if she is engaging with services. The responsibility for adapting quietly shifts onto her.

Such a family in the council flats in the Vale is not uncommon enough to make it stand out. People know which homes are volatile. They avoid such homes. There is a sense that this is what happens, that families get by as best they can. And this sense is reflected in the professionals' responses to Jemma's family. There is concern, but it is tempered by familiarity. There is no sense of urgency because there is no sense of novelty.

Jemma has learned that men's anger is something to be worked around, that endurance is a sign of strength, that silence at times may be a safer option than voice. These are not lessons that are taught; they are lessons that are learned through the way that life has unfolded. Later in life, it would be described as a pattern, not a consequence.

The file does not examine the history of the father's behaviour. It does not seek to understand where it originated or what contributed to it. It simply identifies it and moves on. This is important because it ensures that the response of the system remains narrow in scope. It ensures that the problem continues to be addressed at a surface level.

For Jemma, the impact continues to build and accumulate. There was no single moment that could be used to define the experience of growing up in the presence of fear. There was no clear beginning or end to the fear that she lived with. It was a constant, a background noise that influenced what she considered normal, acceptable and reasonable to expect from others. It taught her that love and harm could exist side by side without cancelling the other out.

When she later indulges in excessive drinking, when she seeks volatile men, when she has trouble settling in one place, all of this is her choice. Her connection with her father is acknowledged and then dismissed. It is her choice.

Her father is still present in the record, but only as a descriptor rather than a participant. Aggressive. Volatile. Alcoholic. It is all so neat and tidy. But the damage is not so neat and tidy. Fear becomes a normal part of Jemma's life, integrated into her understanding of her family and her care. By the time she is 16 years old, this is so normal that she does not even begin to realise it is damaging. It is simply the way things are.

This is where she learns that safety is conditional, that love can shift in an instant, and that sometimes staying is more valued than leaving. This is where she learns all of this and more. This is where she carries it with her long after she leaves the house. This is where she carries it with her long after she leaves her family. It is never spoken of. It is assumed.

The record does not stop to examine any of this. It cannot. It is not built for that. It moves from statement to statement, then on again. The damage does not stay in the file.

It shows up in the child.

Static Child

Before she left, before her name was listed in files or on computer screens, before anyone started counting her absences or measuring her behaviour, she was still. This was before the feeling of calm, before the feeling of peace. It was not a peaceful state, simply a state of being that she learned to exist in without drawing attention to herself.

She learned early on that moving could get her noticed, that getting noticed could mean consequences that she did not understand but wanted to avoid at all costs. She learned to sit without fidgeting, to breathe shallowly so no one would hear, to fix her gaze on one point without looking away. She learned how to be invisible.

No one taught her, no one praised or rewarded her for it. It was simply a part of who she was.

In the house, sound was important. Moving a chair too quickly or closing a cupboard door too loudly could change the tone of the room in a moment. Jemma learned to move quietly, to put her feet down softly on the carpet, to open doors slowly so that they would not squeak in protest. She learned to wait before going into a room, to listen before she entered, to determine whether it was safe to be seen.

Stillness made her presence optional. It allowed her to step back and wait when she sensed that things were not quite right. She could sit on the edge of a bed or on the floor of her own room and wait. Sometimes she waited minutes. Sometimes she waited hours. Until something changed. Until the noise stopped. Until the mood shifted. She learned to wait quietly. This would later be mistaken for patience.

There is no record of this time. No attendance records. No letters home from school that expressed worry. No doctor's appointments that noted her anxiety. This does not mean nothing was happening. It means nothing was being noted. Stillness does not leave a mark.

School, when she went, was a different kind of space. But stillness accompanied her. She learned to sit quietly. To keep her head down. To not make a sound. To not make eye contact. To not ask for help. To not make trouble. This made her easy to control. This made her easy to overlook.

At home, she learned that sometimes, remaining still could shorten an outburst of anger. Sometimes, if she did not react, sometimes if she did not speak, sometimes if she did not move, it would all be over sooner. It was not always true, but it was true enough to become a habit. She started to think, without realising she was doing it, that sometimes stillness could affect what was happening, that sometimes her containment could contain others.

Holding her breath was also a part of this. She did not think to do it, just breathed shallowly until the voices stopped, until she heard the closing of a door or the sound of footsteps moving away, and then breathed again. No one had taught her to do this. It was something that happened through repetition. Something normal. She would struggle to understand in the future why her breathing was constricted or why she was on edge in a room with no noise.

There was always a small hope tied to her stillness. Not a large hope, not a hope tied to any kind of change, but a small hope tied to her being quiet enough, small enough, to ensure nothing happened. That she would not be noticed. That safety was possible through invisibility. This was not something she was consciously aware of. It was something underlying all her actions.

The adults in her life did not comment on her silence in a way that indicated they were worried. Being quiet was being good, was coping. She did not ask for attention, so none was given. And that was good for all parties. The lack of trouble was taken as a sign things were OK.

In the council areas where she grew up, children knew how to make themselves fit into the space they were in. There was an unvoiced understanding that to draw attention to problems was not to solve them. Jemma knew this without anyone needing to explain it to her. Being still was sensible.

At night, when she was in bed, she listened to the sounds of the house. Voices coming from other rooms. The television. Footsteps of someone pacing. She learned to distinguish between regular noise and noise that signalled her to stay awake. Sleep came lightly. She stayed alert even when her eyes were closed. This also went unnoticed.

There were times when she wanted to say something. Times when she wanted to ask for something. Times when she wanted to complain about something that seemed unfair and scary. These times came and went. Silence became better, even if it meant giving something up. She learned to swallow words even before they came out of her mouth.

Nobody sat down with her and asked her how she felt about this period. Nobody asked her what she needed. When experts looked back at this period, they saw a gap, a period when little documentation had been done. This meant stability. This was far from stability. This was merely silence.

Silence followed her outside of home. When she stayed with relatives and friends, she made sure she was not a bother. She cleaned up after herself. She ate whatever she was given. She avoided arguments. This made her welcome. This also meant that no one saw how hard she had to work at being this way.

She learned to control her body. She learned not to make sudden movements. She learned not to make emotional expressions. This also made it difficult for adults to read her. They saw her calm demeanour. They saw her neutrality. They saw her composure. They saw her as unaffected.

There is no single memory that encapsulates this period of her life. It was a series of small moments, each of them insignificant in and of itself: sitting quietly as voices rose in another room; waiting until footsteps moved away before leaving her bedroom; holding her breath through a slammed door, then slowly exhaling once things settled. These moments were not significant in and of themselves. They were simply a part of life.

The hope in stillness was a fragile thing. It was not always rewarded. There were times when things escalated regardless. But it was a habit that continued, simply because it was the only thing she could do that felt within her control. She could not control others. She could only control herself.

When she later began to be described as withdrawn, or unengaged, this period of her life was not taken into account. Her quietness was seen as a lack of interest, or of defiance. The skill she developed to survive was reinterpreted as a problem that needed to be solved.

In hindsight, this period of her life is easy to gloss over. There is no incident to document. There is no drama, no injuries, no behaviour that needs to be acted on. Stillness is simply not noteworthy. It is a period of absence. An absence that allows systems to move on without a second thought.

For Jemma, stillness was a part of how she saw the world. It was a part of how she learned. It taught her that safety was something you could earn, that attention was a danger, that survival was more important than protest. These lessons were learned well. They were lessons that would stay with her, affecting how she would later deal with authority, care and relationships.

Before she was measured, assessed and monitored, she learned how to become invisible in plain sight. That process did not stop when she left home. It stayed with her even when things changed. It influenced how she interacted with adults, how she navigated new spaces, how she evaluated risks.

There are no official records that document this process. It is not in any file. It is not in any report. It is in how she holds herself, how she moves through rooms, how she waits for permission that is never explicitly given. It is in the tension that is still present even when nothing is happening.

The hope that stillness might be misinterpreted as safety was a small one. It was not a hope for happiness or ease. It was a hope that things might continue as they are and that they might not get worse. For a child, that is a hope worth aiming for.

This is the part of Jemma's story that is most difficult to write down because it leaves behind so little evidence. It is not a loud process. It is not a process that demands to be seen. It is a process that simply is, and it informs everything that comes after.

Before Jemma left home, before her name became a word that mattered in meetings and discussions, before adults spoke about her in terms of how to manage and how to control, she learned how to be still. That is a process that mattered. More than anyone knew at the time.

Age of Dismissal

The stillness does not leave her.

Jemma McKay is sixteen years old, and she is already defined within a system as someone who has passed through, rather than someone yet to arrive. Her name is mentioned within minutes and reports, and it has a familiar quality, a quality of longevity, as if she has been around for years rather than months, as if her childhood has been and gone. She is known within social services, and it is put like that, known, as if she is a street corner, a problem address, familiar without being looked at too closely.

The file begins with a summary, a list of offences: drinking, absconding, school attendance, home life. Her age is noted correctly, her date of birth typed neatly at the top of the page, but it does not do her any favours, does not do her any harm, simply does not do anything at all. Her year of birth, nineteen sixty-five, does not make anyone pause, does not make anyone do anything, does not offer her protection.

She lives in a world of Alexandria, Renton, Bonhill. Places that are close enough that buses run regularly through them. Far enough apart that it is possible to disappear for days and no one really knows quite where you are. The world itself is unremarkable. Rows of houses that look just the same. Patches of grass where children kick a ball back and forth until it gets dark. Shops that sell the same things year in and year out. None of it really announces itself as being in trouble.

None of it really announces her. She fades into the background. Fits in. Which makes her rather easy to ignore. Rather easy to talk about in shorthand. Strathclyde Council looms over it all. A name on headed paper. In letters delivered through the post. Occasionally opened. Occasionally left on the table until they curl up at the edges.

The file talks of her. That is the word that is used. Her behaviour. Too much drink for her age. Staying out overnight. Hanging around with older lads. Sometimes men. Being difficult to find. Not being very cooperative. These are all written down. Facts. Pure and unadulterated.

Without the messy bits that lie underneath. Very little is said of her home life beyond what has been labelled. The domestic abuse. The alcohol abuse by her father. The police calls. These are mentioned and passed over, as if their very presence is reason enough. The environment itself is dealt with quickly, reduced to a few lines. Enough said. Enough done. What matters is what she does, where she goes, who she is with, how often she does not turn up, how often she is late.

She is talked about in meetings she does not attend. Adults sit in rooms, discussing her progress, her demeanour, her lack of engagement. Her absence becomes part of her character, not something to question.

When she does attend, when she sits on a plastic chair in an office, often in Dumbarton, often with a social worker she knows too well.

She answers carefully. Enough, but not too much. There is always the sense that she is being measured rather than helped, that the conversation is less about understanding and more about recording. She knows how to respond. She knows which words open things up and which ones close them down.

Her father appears in the record in fragments, usually tied to incidents. He is described as volatile, aggressive when drinking. The police appear often.

There is no space to describe how this shapes a child, how it teaches you to leave before things escalate, how it keeps you alert to mood and movement. The harm is acknowledged but not explored. It sits as background, something that explains her behaviour without altering the response to it.

Now she is sixteen, and she is expected to manage herself. The language used around her is the language of choice. She chooses to drink. She chooses to stay away. She chooses risk. The words suggest control, as if these decisions come from stability. There is little curiosity about what she is choosing between, or what staying might mean.

She moves from house to house, staying with friends, sometimes with people she barely knows. Sofas become beds. Nights blur into days. She learns to take up as little space as possible, to accept what is offered without asking for more. The men around her are older. They offer drink, somewhere to stay, attention that passes for safety. The file does not explore this. It is mentioned just enough to register concern, not enough to act. Her vulnerability is noted, then overlooked.

School attendance is poor. Days are missed. This is labelled disengagement. There is no discussion of what it takes to attend school when you have not slept, when you are managing adult situations with a child's capacity, when being there means answering questions you cannot answer honestly. The expectation remains the same: she should comply, she should understand, she should try harder. Responsibility rests with her.

When professionals talk about her, there is already a tiredness in the tone. She is difficult. She does not engage. There is an assumption that support has been offered and refused, though what that support looks like is rarely clear. Advice is given. Appointments are made. She does not always attend. This becomes evidence of unwillingness, rather than a sign that something in the approach is not working.

She is sixteen, but she knows these systems. She knows offices, forms, repeated questions. She knows that honesty can create problems, that saying too much can lead to consequences she cannot control. She learns to keep things vague. To appear capable. To minimise fear. To laugh things off. Her ability to endure is taken as proof that she is coping.

The file does not dwell on her feelings. It does not ask what it is like to move between places, to live as both child and adult depending on what is required. It does not ask what she wants, beyond broad statements about things improving. Improvement remains undefined. It allows agreement without obligation.

There are moments when concern sharpens. A missed appointment. A call from school. A police incident. Then it fades. The system responds and settles again. There is no sustained urgency. Her life continues in the gaps.

She moves through this with both resistance and exhaustion. She is used to being talked about, reduced to summary. She does not expect help. She expects judgement. She expects to be told what she should have done differently without being shown how. She gives enough to avoid escalation and withholds enough to retain control.

The communities she moves through are small. People know each other. Reputations travel. She knows how she is seen: trouble, drink, risk. These labels arrive before she does. By the time she enters a room, the version of her that matters is already there.

Her age remains a technicality. Sixteen defines thresholds, categories, services. In practice, it changes little. She is expected to carry adult responsibility and child compliance at the same time. The contradiction goes unspoken, and it shapes every interaction.

Strathclyde Council remains present but distant. Letters arrive. Meetings are scheduled. There is movement on paper, even when her life feels still. Support happens around her, sometimes including her, often missing her. She becomes something to be managed rather than someone involved.

There is no defining moment here. No single crisis that forces change. There is accumulation instead: missed days, nights away, incidents that matter but do not shift anything. Without a turning point, everything continues.

She is still sixteen in the record and far older in experience. She has learned how to exist within systems without trusting them, how to survive without depending on anyone. These are not recognised as adaptations. They are read as attitude.

She is present in reports and absent in decisions. A child in definition, an adult in expectation. Known to services, a phrase that suggests care but often functions as record-keeping. Her environment remains largely unexamined. Her behaviour remains the focus.

Her story is already being written.

There is little space for anything else to happen.

Not Departure

It is not announced. There is no final argument, no suitcase packed with intent. It happens in small shifts that are easy to miss at the time and obvious only later. One night away becomes two. Two becomes a pattern. Jemma does not think she has left home so much as she realises, one day, that she is rarely there and no one has come looking. The door remains open, but nothing behind it has changed. Only the same tension she learned to manage by staying quiet.

At first, she is only staying overnight. A friend's house in Alexandria where no one asks too many questions. A floor in Renton after a night that runs late. She brings little because she expects to go back. A change of clothes. Borrowed make-up she will not return. It is occasional, at first. Then less so.

Sofas become beds. Sleep becomes shallow, shaped by what is happening around her. She learns to wake quickly, to gather herself without fuss. Mornings blur. Someone always needs the sofa back. She leaves without complaint, without drawing attention. She leaves without being missed. More than that, she has already left.

There are always parties. Always somewhere that fills the space between needing somewhere to stay. Alcohol is easy to find. It dulls things, stretches time. Nights run into mornings without clear edges. She learns to function on little rest. The fatigue does not go away. It is carried.

Older men become visible over time. At first, they sit at the edges. Friends of friends. Someone with a car. Someone with a flat. They offer lifts, drinks, somewhere to stay. It is framed as kindness. Jemma understands quickly that nothing is free. She also understands that saying no carries its own cost. She weighs it constantly. Where will I stay? How will I get there? What will this cost me?

Later, it will be called grooming. Or choice. At the time, it is calculation. If she stays, something is expected. If she leaves, something else is expected. She does not name it. Naming it would require a position she does not feel she has. It is not presented as harm. It is presented as arrangement.

Later, it will be called a lifestyle. The word is neat. It suggests preference. It suggests options. It leaves no space for pressure or necessity.

For Jemma, it is logistics. Where can she go? How long can she stay? How much can she drink to keep things smooth? How little can she say?

School fades without a clear end. Days become weeks. Letters may be sent. Calls may be made. They do not always reach her. When she does attend, she feels out of place. Tired. Out of step. Teachers notice sometimes. When they ask, she shrugs it off. She has learned how to do that.

Home becomes somewhere she passes through rather than stays. She goes back occasionally to collect something or to check in. Nothing has changed. Nothing has softened. Her absence has altered nothing. It confirms what she already knows.

Independence is assigned to her quickly. She is sixteen and moving around on her own, so it is assumed she knows what she is doing. The assumption reduces responsibility elsewhere. If she is independent, she does not require the same level of oversight. If she is choosing to stay away, then she must be managing.

This suits systems that are already stretched. Concern can exist without action. Responsibility can sit with her. When things go wrong, it can be said that she put herself there.

Jemma learns to read adults carefully. She knows who will escalate things if they hear too much and who will let things pass if she keeps it vague. She talks about friends without naming them. About staying over without saying where. It is not calculated in a formal way. It is instinct. A way to hold some control where there is very little.

Money becomes a problem. She has little, and it goes quickly. Lifts cost something. Drinks cost something. Staying somewhere costs something, even when it is not said. Often, the cost is sex. Sometimes it is tolerating what makes her uncomfortable. She learns to disconnect just enough to get through it. It is not named as exploitation. It is survival.

In the estates around the Vale, this kind of drifting is not unusual. People know girls who move between houses, who fall out of school, who start drinking early. It is seen as sad rather than urgent. Jemma stays within that line.

She disappears in plain sight. People see her out. At parties. Getting into cars. This visibility creates the impression she is accounted for. In reality, no one is responsible for her. No one knows where she will be sleeping. This is not recognised as risk.

The language around her shifts. Streetwise. Worldly. Mature for her age. These sound like observations, but they function as justification. If she is capable, intervention feels less necessary.

There are moments when things catch up with her. Nights with nowhere to go. Situations that go further than she expected. These moments are not spoken about. She absorbs them and carries on. There is no space to process them, and no expectation that she should.

Later, she will be asked why she did not go home. Why she did not ask for help. These questions assume home was safe and help was available. They do not account for what it means to return to something unchanged, or to ask for help when nothing has shifted before.

Leaving is not freedom. It is exchange. One set of risks for another. Some feel easier to manage because they are predictable. That does not make them safe. It makes them familiar.

The distance between Jemma and support widens. Appointments are missed because she does not know where she will be, or because attending feels pointless. When contact happens, she says she is fine. Staying with friends. Managing. This is accepted. It fits the version of her already forming.

The erosion continues. Of relationships. Of expectation. Of support. The longer she is away, the harder it becomes to imagine returning in any meaningful way. Leaving is no longer about where she is. It is about what she no longer expects.

Later, this period is reduced to a few lines. Left home. Sofa surfing. Drinking. Risky relationships. The detail disappears. The effort of each day is lost.

By the time services look more closely, this way of living is established. It is no longer temporary. It is a pattern. One that is then read as character rather than circumstance.

Leaving is framed as growing up. As independence. As responsibility. It allows absence of care to be reinterpreted as self-sufficiency.

For Jemma, it is motion without direction. Adaptation without support. Survival without expectation of care.

She leaves home without leaving what home taught her.

The erosion continues.

Relocation

The decision to go to England does not appear as a decision. It appears as a change of location, a brief entry that she has gone south, that she is staying with someone, that she has been out of touch for a time. There is no entry that describes how this came about or what led up to it. It simply appears as a fact. She is no longer where she was expected to be, and that fact is noted without any sense of alarm.

Jemma does not announce that she is leaving. She tells someone, maybe two. A friend she is staying with. A person who gives her a lift. The details are vague because the plan is vague. She knows she is going somewhere else. She does not know for how long. England is near enough to feel within reach and far enough to matter. A few hours on the motorway and she is outside the council that knows her name.

She crosses a border. It does not feel like anything. There is no sense of occasion. No checkpoint. The landscape shifts slowly. Place names change. Accents change. Nothing marks it as important, even though it is.

She is still sixteen. No one checks. No one asks. No one calls ahead. She arrives somewhere new and is taken at face value. This feels easier than the kind of attention she is used to. She stays where she is told she can stay. She adjusts quickly. She has learned how to do that.

Back in West Dunbartonshire, the file is updated. She is noted to be in England. This is not escalated. There is no welfare check. No referral across the border. Her absence is recorded, but not acted on. She is out of area, which means she is out of remit. Responsibility thins.

Distance works like this. Once you cross a boundary, the sense of obligation weakens. No one decides she does not matter. There is simply no clear way to keep hold of her. She becomes someone else's responsibility in theory, and no one's in practice.

What she says is accepted. She is staying with friends. She is safe. She will be in touch. It is written down and left there. There is an assumption that if something were wrong, she would say, that she would know how to say it.

In England, her days fall into a loose pattern. She stays indoors more. She spends time with people she has only just met but now depends on. She learns the rules of new houses quickly. Where to sit. When to speak. When to leave the room. The skills she learned earlier make this easier than it should be. She does not expect comfort. She expects tolerance.

Money is scarce. It always is. She contributes where she can, in ways that do not need to be discussed. She drinks when drinks are there. She stays quiet when things feel tense. She makes do. Later, this will be read as competence.

There is no school here. No expectation that there should be. No one checks if she is enrolled anywhere. Education drops away without resistance. It is not marked as absence. It looks like continuation.

Time loses its shape. Without appointments or structure, days blur. She sleeps when she can. Eats when food is there. Waits for other people to decide what happens next. This does not feel strange. It feels familiar.

Back home, there is a brief attempt at contact. A call. No answer. A note added. Then it settles. Her absence becomes normal. The system adjusts around it rather than responding to it.

No one contacts services in England. There is no handover. The assumption sits underneath everything: she chose to go, so she must be managing.

Jemma does not feel free. She feels exposed. There is no safety net here. No one who knows her history. No one who might notice something is wrong. At the same time, there is relief in not being watched, not being questioned, not being reduced to a problem.

She has occasional contact with people back home. She does not know what to say. There is no clear version of this time. She is not better. She is not worse. She is just elsewhere.

Home feels distant. Not just in miles, but in meaning. Nothing there has changed. Going back would mean stepping back into the same conditions. Staying away feels easier, even with the risk.

The file reflects this. Entries shorten. Updates slow. Her name appears less often. Not because concern has gone, but because there is little to record. Absence produces very little paperwork.

There is an assumption she will come back. That this is temporary. That it can be waited out. That assumption makes inaction feel reasonable.

In England, things happen that would have raised concern if they had been seen. Arguments. Drinking that goes too far. Nights where she feels unsafe. These moments stay with her. There is no way to pass them on, and no expectation that doing so would change anything.

She learns that being out of sight also means being out of reach. If something happens here, it happens without anyone responsible knowing. She becomes more careful. More aware. She manages herself.

The people around her do not ask her age, or they do and do not treat it as important. She looks older. She carries herself in a way that suggests experience. That is enough.

Back in West Dunbartonshire, her absence fades into the background. Other cases take priority. Nothing escalates. Nothing interrupts. The system does what it is built to do. It records and waits. Distance allows something to be known without being acted on. It spreads responsibility thin enough that no one has to hold it.

She stays longer than she meant to. There is no clear reason for staying. Only no reason to leave. When she comes back, the time away is not examined closely. It is noted as a gap. Questions are asked lightly. There is no real account of what happened.

There is an assumption that if something serious had occurred, it would have come to light.

It does not.

The case continues as if the time away were a pause rather than a rupture. England does not carry forward. What happens there does not shape what comes next. It sits outside the frame. For Jemma, it confirms something she has been learning for a long time: that it is possible to disappear, that absence is possible, that distance works.

Distance works. It always has.

Returning

Jemma comes back without ceremony. There is no handover, no meeting arranged to coincide with her return. No sense of closure before anything else begins. She reappears in the same places she left, the same schemes, the same routes between Alexandria, Renton, Bonhill. People notice briefly, then move on. Her return is expected. Expected makes it unremarkable.

The system responds in much the same way. Her name reappears after an absence. Weeks of nothing, then another entry, picking up where it left off.

The gap is visible, but it is not questioned. There are no queries about where she went, who she was with, what happened while she was away. She is simply present. She attends another meeting. Home visits are arranged. Everything is familiar. The words are familiar. The concerns are familiar.

Drinking.

Attendance.

Engagement.

There is no acknowledgement that she crossed a border at sixteen and lived outside oversight. No pause. No interest. It settles back into place, as if it had only been waiting.

Jemma knows this. She knows she will not be asked to account for the time away. There is comfort in that, and something else. What she did, what she saw, what she felt belongs to her. It will stay there. She does not offer it.

The questions are practical. Where are you staying? Are you back with family or friends? Are you planning to remain in the area? She answers carefully. Enough, but not too much. Detail draws attention.

There is no assessment to mark the return. No reconsideration of risk. The assumption is simple. If she is back, things have settled. Return becomes resolution.

Appointments resume, or attempts to resume them do. If she misses one, it is recorded as before. If she attends, it is recorded positively. The pattern continues. The system does not change. It smooths the gap into something that reads as continuous.

The continuity is false. She does not name it that way, but she feels it. Something has been left out. What happened in England sits outside the version of her life that is written down. It does not count because it does not fit.

There is talk of her return as an opportunity. Now she is back, things might improve. The optimism rests on proximity alone.

Home has not changed. The same tensions. The same patterns. Her father's drinking and aggression remain. The house feels exactly as it did before. Familiarity is taken as stability.

There is an expectation that she will return to work or training. The conversation circles back to attendance. She agrees. She does not argue. Agreement is easier than explaining how far away that feels.

No one asks how she feels about being back. No one asks if she feels safe. Those questions have fallen away. She is treated as someone who manages herself. Her age is still written down. It does nothing.

The gap in the file is not treated as concern. It becomes background. Something that happened and ended. The behaviour remains the focus. The experience is left alone.

Jemma understands that returning has closed something rather than opened it. When she was away, she was out of sight. That carried risk, but it also meant less attention. Back home, the attention returns. She adjusts. She returns to what keeps it manageable.

The language around her does not change. She is still hard to engage. Still making bad choices. The time away alters nothing. It is as if it never happened.

Her absence is mentioned briefly in a meeting, framed as time away from the area. The phrasing removes risk. No one challenges it. The conversation moves on.

Jemma knows the story is not about what she experienced. It is about what is written. She does not try to correct it.

Her return also makes something else clear. Services are bounded by geography. When she left, responsibility fell away. Now she is back, it returns without reflection.

Life continues in the same uneven rhythm. Nights out. Drinking. Moving between houses. These are treated as ongoing concerns, not escalation. This is the baseline now.

There is frustration at times. Why did she leave? Why does she keep putting herself at risk? The questions assume choice. They overlook what was available to her, and what was not done.

Her return becomes reassurance. She came back. She is fine.

The file continues to grow. New entries sit alongside old ones. The gap remains a blank space rather than a break. This creates continuity. It suggests nothing significant was interrupted.

For Jemma, the message is clear. She left. She came back. Nothing changed. No questions. No shift. The lesson settles quietly.

The schemes look the same. The streets, the shops, the routes. Nothing marks the time that has passed. The system mirrors this. It continues as before.

Returning does not bring closure. It brings resumption. The thread is picked up and flattened. What happened in between is left out. That is how continuity is made.

Jemma moves forward with what is not written down. The system moves forward with what it already knows. They move alongside each other without meeting.

This is how the return is handled. Quietly. Efficiently. Without pause.

The moment that might have made a difference passes unnoticed.

The story continues.

And for Jemma, something settles into place. What happens to her only matters when it can be seen.

Visible and Unseen

The pregnancy comes to light late, and not in a way that feels personal. It surfaces during a routine check, asked because it sits on a form, not because anyone has noticed anything different. Jemma does not volunteer the information. She answers when prompted. There is a brief pause as it lands, and then something shifts. Quietly, but straight away.

Concern softens into care. Voices drop a little. Questions lose their edge. Where there were once reminders and cautions, there are now offers and suggestions. Even the way people talk about her changes. She is no longer just a young woman making bad choices. She is a pregnant young woman. That difference matters.

Someone says there is still time to get support in place, even though there really is not. Dates are adjusted. Missed appointments are reframed as understandable. Drinking is talked about as something to work on, not something to confront. The focus moves away from behaviour and towards outcome. The outcome now feels real, something that can be named.

Jemma listens. She recognises the shift. She knows what it means when attention gathers like this instead of slipping away. She answers carefully, says she wants to do things properly. For now, that is enough. Wanting counts for more than what she can manage.

No one dwells on how she did not realise sooner, or what that might say. The delay is acknowledged, then folded into urgency. It becomes a reason to act quickly, to put things in place. The pregnancy gives her life a kind of structure it has not had before.

Referrals start to come up. Midwives. Health visitors. Support for young parents. The names are spoken with certainty. Leaflets are handed over. Appointments are booked. Things begin to move.

People speak to her as if she is both delicate and capable at the same time. The balance is not perfect, but it is deliberate. The aim is to keep her involved, to help without pushing her away. It is different from before, and she notices.

Housing comes up again. Where are you staying? The question carries more weight now. Stability becomes important. There is talk of finding somewhere suitable, of putting support in place. It feels new. Before, where she lived had been treated as a result of her choices. Now it is treated as risk.

The pregnancy reshapes how her past is seen. The drinking, the drifting, the missed appointments are still there, but they are repositioned. Things that can change. Things that can improve. There is optimism in that shift, an assumption that pregnancy will bring things into line, that a baby will change everything.

Jemma does not argue. She understands how this works. Optimism brings help. It brings patience. It creates a version of her that people can invest in. She steps into that version carefully.

She is encouraged to attend antenatal appointments. She agrees. Turning up becomes a sign of engagement. When she attends, it is noted. When she does not, people follow up rather than pull back. The response is softer now.

People ask how she feels. She says she is OK, getting used to it. That is accepted. There is not much space for doubt. Pregnancy is framed as opportunity. Uncertainty is redirected.

Her family situation is raised again. The same issues, seen differently. There is talk about reducing stress, setting boundaries, keeping things calm. The advice assumes she has more control than she does, but the assumption stays in place. A turning point begins to take shape. No one says it outright, but it sits underneath everything. This could be where things change. The system leans into that idea, offers something that looks like direction.

Jemma feels the pressure of it. More is at stake now. What she does will be read differently. At the same time, there is something else. Attention that feels closer, more holding than watching. She is not used to it.

Her age comes up again, but it lands differently this time. Being young now means support, not criticism. She is offered services designed for people like her. She is told others have managed. It reassures, but it also sets a standard.

The pregnancy gives her something to organise around. Scans. Dates. Milestones. Points to aim for. She starts shaping her days around them. It gives her direction, even if it is not one she chose. There are conversations about stopping drinking. They are careful, centred on the baby, on care rather than rules. She says she will try. That is enough to be marked as progress.

She makes it to more appointments than she misses. When she shows up, she is described as engaged. She listens, asks questions. These details are written down. They build a picture of improvement.

What sits underneath is harder to see. Where she stays is still uncertain. Money is still tight. Relationships are still unstable. These things are noted, but they do not take centre stage. The pregnancy does.

There is a sense that time is short. Things need to come together quickly. Plans are talked about, sometimes without much detail. There is confidence that support will lead to stability, that things will fall into place.

Out in public, people treat her differently now. Kinder. More patient. Less quick to judge. She notices. She also knows it depends on her staying within the role she has been given.

She tries, in the ways she can. She turns up when possible. She cuts back where she is able. She presents herself as cooperative. The effort is real, even if it is not steady.

The system responds to that. Notes become more positive. The language shifts. There is talk about the future, about what happens after the baby arrives. It becomes something that can be planned. There is not much room for fear in these conversations. Fear about birth. About what comes after. About whether she can keep this going. The focus stays on practical steps.

The pregnancy becomes the lens for everything. It reshapes her past and defines what comes next, bringing a kind of order to things that did not have it.

For Jemma, this is a period of being seen more clearly and watched more closely. Support and pressure sit side by side. She carries both.

The system needs this to be a turning point, and it leans into that belief. It lets that belief shape what happens. Whether she can live up to it is not explored. For now, intention is enough. Showing up is enough. The pregnancy rewrites her story. It offers the possibility of something better. The language reflects that. Softer. More hopeful.

This is where hope settles into the record.

It shapes what comes next.

Jemma moves forward within that attention, aware of what it gives and what it asks of her. She knows, even if she never says it, that turning points do not hold on their own.

They have to be carried.

Performing Stability

Jemma attends the appointments by herself. This becomes evident, sometimes clearly, sometimes by the absence of anyone else sitting beside her. Occasionally she is late. She signs in, sits down, and waits to be called. No one has to chase her down the close or phone to remind her where she should be. In a system built around missed appointments and non-attendance, this is noted as something that matters.

Jemma listens to what the professionals have to say. When they speak, she focuses on them, nods at the right moments, asks for clarification when she does not understand. She does not interrupt or argue. She has learned that listening draws less attention than defending herself. It is also more effective. It reads as engagement.

When she asks questions, they are practical. What happens next? Who will she see after this? What is expected before the next appointment? These are not emotional questions. They are about process. About what she needs to know to move through the situation she is in. She wants to understand the rules.

One midwife comments that she seems motivated. A support worker notes that she understands the importance of attending. Another writes that she asks appropriate questions and appears keen to do well. These sentences are small, but they carry weight. They move between reports, shaping how people speak about her before they meet her.

This belief matters. It affects conversations held in rooms she does not enter. When her name is mentioned, there is less frustration. Less talk of non-compliance. She is described as trying. Trying sits carefully between success and failure. It allows for imperfection without condemnation.

Jemma feels the difference, even if it is not said outright. Missed calls are returned. Explanations are accepted. She is given the benefit of the doubt. This makes it easier to keep attending. The relationship becomes something closer to reciprocal.

She attends alone. No partner. No parent. This is noted, but not as a concern. Her independence is assumed. She manages her appointments, her paperwork, her travel. It is framed as a strength.

Inside the rooms where she is seen, she is composed. She keeps her emotions contained. No tears. No visible panic. This is read as coping. No one asks what it costs her to maintain that control. They respond to what they can see.

She takes the leaflets and puts them in her bag. She does not always read them, but she keeps them. They show that information has been given. They also carry expectation. Eat properly. Avoid alcohol. Rest. Attend. Instructions built on a level of stability she does not always have, but does not name.

When she misses an appointment, there is follow-up. A call. A message. The absence is not immediately treated as failure. It is treated as a setback. The distinction matters. It allows her to return.

One morning, she nearly does not go.

The night before had been long. Shouting in the flat below. Someone hammering on a door that was not hers but close enough to keep her awake. She had not slept. She had not eaten. The idea of sitting under fluorescent lights, answering questions she could not afford to answer, felt unbearable.

She stands outside the clinic for ten minutes. Smokes half a cigarette.

Then she goes in. Smiles. Apologises for being late. Blames the bus. The receptionist nods. The explanation is ordinary enough to pass. Inside, the midwife asks if she has been taking her folic acid. Jemma nods. She has not. She cannot remember when she last did.

The midwife smiles, but the look lingers a moment longer than usual. Not quite suspicion. Not quite concern. Jemma cannot name it, only that something has been noticed. She leaves quickly and does not take a leaflet on the way out.

The system records attendance. The file shows she was there. For Jemma, it is the closest she has come to stepping outside the version of her being written down.

She notices that people speak about her future with cautious optimism. They talk about what she will need when the baby arrives. Support. Routine. Stability. It feels unreal. Her life rarely extends beyond the next few days. Still, she listens. Agreement keeps doors open.

She is careful when she speaks about where she is staying. She mentions friends, but does not elaborate. She says she is managing. She avoids naming instability directly. Too much honesty risks intervention. Too little risks dismissal. She stays in between.

Professionals respond to that balance. They see someone willing to engage. Someone making an effort. They want to support that. Their approach softens. This is how belief takes hold.

Her attendance becomes a reference point. Later, when concerns arise, someone will say she attended well during pregnancy, that she engaged, that she asked the right questions. These details will carry forward.

At the time, Jemma experiences the process as demanding but manageable. The structure helps. Knowing where she needs to be, and when, gives shape to her days. The expectations are clear, even if meeting them takes effort she does not name.

She does not speak much about how she feels. Partly because she is not asked in a way that allows it. Partly because she does not have the language. She can describe actions. Feelings are less certain.

The professionals do not push this. They focus on what can be observed. Attendance. Engagement. Compliance.

A note appears in the file: Jemma appears receptive to advice. It is a positive assessment. It suggests openness. Potential. It fits the narrative forming around her.

That narrative matters. It influences thresholds. Later decisions will draw on this period. She tried. She engaged. She showed insight. These points will soften how future concerns are read.

Jemma does not know this at the time. She only knows things feel different, and that she should hold on to that for as long as she can. She keeps attending, even when she is tired, even when it is inconvenient, even when she would rather not. She understands that being seen trying matters.

She is praised occasionally. Small things. Well done for coming in. Good to see you again. The words land more heavily than intended. They confirm that her effort is visible.

No one asks how she manages it. No one asks what it takes to get there.

She begins to recognise certain professionals as predictable. Not safe, exactly, but consistent. She knows how they will respond. That predictability helps.

When she speaks about the baby, her language is careful. She talks about doing her best. About wanting things to be OK. It fits the version of her taking shape. It is received well.

Being seen as engaged becomes self-reinforcing. Because she is believed to be trying, she is treated as worth investing in.

It does not change the instability underneath her life. It creates a buffer. It buys time. It delays more intrusive action. For now, that is seen as success.

Jemma knows she is being assessed, even when it is not obvious. She adjusts. Not as strategy, but as survival in a system that responds to certain signals.

She leaves appointments with relief and tension mixed together. Relief that she attended. That nothing went wrong. Tension because she has to keep it going. Trying is not a single act. It is ongoing. The belief that she is engaged is written down. Repeated. Shared. It will shape what comes next more than anyone realises.

For now, she keeps showing up. She listens. She asks sensible questions. She does what she understands she is meant to do. The effort is real, even if it is fragile.

Trying becomes her role. The way she is understood. The way she is measured. That will matter later, when things begin to slip and explanations are needed. For now, the belief holds. She is engaged. She is trying. And because of that, the system responds as if things are moving in the right direction.

When she speaks about the baby, her language is careful. She talks about doing her best. About wanting things to be OK. It fits the version of her taking shape. It is received well.

Being seen as engaged becomes self-reinforcing. Because she is believed to be trying, she is treated as worth investing in.

It does not change the instability underneath her life. It creates a buffer. It buys time. It delays more intrusive action. For now, that is seen as success.

Jemma knows she is being assessed, even when it is not obvious. She adjusts. Not as strategy, but as survival in a system that responds to certain signals.

She leaves appointments with relief and tension mixed together. Relief that she attended. That nothing went wrong. Tension because she has to keep it going. Trying is not a single act. It is ongoing. The belief that she is engaged is written down. Repeated. Shared. It will shape what comes next more than anyone realises.

For now, she keeps showing up. She listens. She asks sensible questions. She does what she understands she is meant to do. The effort is real, even if it is fragile.

Trying becomes her role. The way she is understood. The way she is measured. That will matter later, when things begin to slip and explanations are needed. For now, the belief holds. She is engaged. She is trying. And because of that, the system responds as if things are moving in the right direction.

Promises

The plans begin to appear once it is agreed that Jemma is engaging. The agreement does not arrive all at once. It settles through repetition. Attendance noted. Questions asked. Tone cooperative. By the time a meeting is arranged to bring things together, the conclusion is already in place. She is someone worth planning for.

The first plan is discussed in a small room, around a table that has held many versions of the same conversation. Papers are spread out. Names and roles are clarified. Someone says this is about support, not scrutiny. Someone else adds that the aim is to have everything in place before the baby arrives. The language is careful. Reassuring. Jemma listens.

Goals are set early. Attend appointments. Reduce drinking. Secure stable accommodation. Engage with support services. They are written down in bullet points that make them feel manageable. Each one is reasonable on its own. Together, they create a picture of improvement that works on paper.

Jemma is asked if the goals feel realistic. She says yes. She has learned that saying no complicates things. No one asks what would make them realistic. The assumption is that support already exists, or can be arranged. That assumption allows the plan to move forward.

Someone notes that Jemma has shown insight into her situation. This is based on her attendance and her agreement with the plan. Insight becomes something attributed to her, rather than something tested. It reassures the room. It suggests she understands what is at stake.

The instability in her life is acknowledged, but softened. Housing is described as temporary rather than precarious. Relationships are described as complex rather than unsafe. Drinking is framed as something she is reducing rather than something she relies on. Each version leans towards what is workable.

Jemma sits quietly while this happens. She hears her life summarised in language that does not quite fit and does not correct it. She knows the plan depends on a certain version of events. Challenging it would slow things down. She needs things to keep moving.

Timelines are introduced. When the next review will take place. What should be in place by then. The baby's due date sits underneath everything, shaping urgency without being directly named.

The plan is written up and circulated. It looks tidy. It reads well. It suggests coordination and purpose. It also spreads responsibility thinly. Everyone has a role. No one holds it alone.

Jemma is given a copy. She folds it and puts it in her bag. She does not read it closely. She already knows the outline. Attend. Cooperate. Try.

Promises are made, though rarely called that. Someone says they will look into housing. Someone else says they will make a referral. Another suggests things will be easier once services are fully involved. The statements are sincere. They are also vague enough to be difficult to follow up.

Concerns still surface. A missed appointment. Reports of drinking. An argument in a place she is staying. These are raised briefly, then folded back into the plan as issues to monitor. Monitoring becomes the default response.

While the plan is in place, Jemma is understood as moving forward. That understanding gives her room to continue, even when things do not improve in the ways expected.

She knows the plan depends on how she presents. She needs to keep attending. Keep agreeing. Keep appearing motivated. The effort required to sustain this is not acknowledged. It is assumed.

Professionals talk about consistency. About building trust. About working together. The phrases are familiar. They settle easily in the room.

At one meeting, someone says pregnancy often helps young women settle. The comment is not challenged. It fits the narrative already forming.

The paperwork grows. Each update refers back to the original goals. Attendance becomes evidence. Agreement becomes compliance. The plan begins to carry itself.

There is less talk about her past now. The focus turns forward. What matters is what she will do next, not what she has lived through.

Jemma is thanked for her cooperation. She is told she is doing well. The praise reinforces the idea that she is responsible for the plan working.

As weeks pass, timelines stretch. Housing takes longer than expected. Referrals are delayed. Appointments are rearranged. None of this is framed as failure. It is described as process. Jemma waits.

In meetings, optimism is repeated. She has been attending well. She is engaging. By the time the plan is reviewed, it has already shaped how she is seen. She is no longer just a young woman with instability in her history. She is a young woman with a plan. That distinction offers protection.

For now, the promises hold. They allow the system to move forward with confidence. Jemma moves with it, aware that the ground beneath her remains uneven, even if the paperwork suggests otherwise. Hope settles where caution might have been.

It is well intentioned.

It is also fragile.

Appointments

Attendance is described as adequate. Engagement is variable but acceptable. The phrases recur, carried forward with new dates. They do a particular kind of work. They hold the line between concern and action. Enough is being done to keep things moving. Not enough has gone wrong to require anything different.

Jemma attends many of the appointments. Not all. Enough. She turns up to midwifery visits, to health checks, to meetings arranged by services that now have a stake in her pregnancy. Sometimes she is early and waits. Sometimes she is late and apologises. Sometimes she cancels at the last minute or does not answer her phone. Each outcome is recorded. None of them are decisive on their own.

On some days, she arrives already exhausted. She has slept badly. She has moved between places. She has had arguments that stay in her body even when the room she is sitting in feels calm. She does not explain this. She answers questions briefly. Keeps things neutral. It is read as reserved rather than overwhelmed.

Jemma learns how far that flexibility extends. She misses an appointment and receives a reminder. She misses another and is asked if everything is OK.

She says it is.

Nothing changes.

When she engages more actively, when she asks questions or follows up on something suggested, it is noted positively. These moments stand out. They offset quieter visits and missed ones. They help maintain the overall assessment of acceptable engagement.

There are appointments she dreads more than others. Meetings with several professionals. Reviews where her situation is discussed in broader terms. She sits through them, aware of how she is being read. Patience is justified. Risk remains theoretical. As long as she keeps turning up some of the time, progress can be assumed.

There are days when she feels close to disengaging entirely. On those days, she weighs it carefully. She knows one missed appointment will not collapse things. Several might. She adjusts accordingly.

The language used to describe her engagement allows for that adjustment. Variable but acceptable creates space. It does not require consistency. Only that things do not visibly worsen. Professionals talk about reminder texts and flexible times. Attendance becomes the issue to solve.

Jemma does not explain why attending is difficult. She knows explanations invite solutions she may not want, or cannot manage. She keeps her reasons to herself. The gaps are filled by assumptions that are easier to hold.

As the pregnancy progresses, appointments increase. More dates. More places to be. More chances to be marked present or absent. When she attends, she is described as pleasant. Cooperative. Polite. When her attention drifts, it is read as tiredness. Pregnancy provides an explanation that requires no further questioning.

Engagement is also measured by what she does not do. She does not argue. She does not become hostile. She does not refuse outright. These absences are recorded as positives.

When professionals meet without her, attended and missed appointments are considered together. The conclusion holds. Engagement remains variable but acceptable. No reassessment follows.

Appointments continue. They accumulate in the file as evidence of ongoing work. Taken together, they form a picture of sufficient engagement.

For Jemma, this period is defined by effort that is largely unseen and outcomes that remain unclear. She knows she is doing enough to stay within tolerance. She does not know if it will ever be enough to change anything.

Adequate.

Variable but acceptable.

Nothing shifts.

Warnings Reclassified

The missed visits do not arrive all at once. They appear gradually, spaced far enough apart to be explained away. One appointment is missed, the next attended. Another is cancelled late, followed by a call apologising. The pattern does not announce itself. It waits.

Alcohol is mentioned quietly. It enters as a side note rather than a concern. Someone asks how things are going. Jemma answers honestly enough to suggest she has not stopped completely. The response is measured. Advice is repeated. A note is made. No one sharpens their tone. The mention sits lightly on the page.

Excuses are logged without challenge. She says she forgot, got the day wrong, the bus did not come. These explanations are familiar, plausible. They are accepted because they fit the framework already in place. Each one stands alone. None are joined up.

Jemma is tired. The tiredness sits behind her eyes and does not lift when she rests. It makes concentration difficult, dates harder to hold onto. She does not describe it this way. She does not have the language. She moves more slowly. Answers a moment later than expected.

She continues to attend some appointments. When she does, she makes an effort to look presentable enough to avoid comment. Keeps her voice steady. She knows how thin the line is.

When someone asks why she missed the last visit, she apologises. Offers a brief explanation. Does not elaborate. The apology is accepted, but not examined. The conversation moves on. The slip is treated as resolved. The notes reflect variable engagement. The phrase appears again, adjusted slightly to match recent attendance. A suggestion is added that additional support may help. The tone remains calm. Nothing is framed as serious enough to disrupt the plan.

Each missed visit is treated as its own event. No one stops to list them together. No one draws a line between tiredness, missed appointments, alcohol and housing instability. Each piece is held separately. That makes it easier to manage.

Jemma senses a shift. The patience is still there, but it asks more of her now. She works harder to appear cooperative. Agrees with suggestions. Thanks people for their time. Rarely pushes back.

Some days, attending feels impossible. Getting up, getting dressed, travelling across town to sit in a waiting room requires energy she does not have. On those days, she weighs it carefully. Sometimes she does not go. Sometimes she goes anyway and sits quietly, counting the minutes until she can leave.

Alcohol appears again in the notes. Still lightly. Something to be aware of. No escalation. The assumption is that she understands the need to reduce it. That understanding is carried forward from earlier conversations, rather than tested now.

Jemma feels the pressure to keep the story intact. The story is that she is trying, that she is engaged, that she is moving forward. Each slip strains it slightly, but not enough to break it. She learns how much strain it can take.

She does not talk about the effort of being watched while managing daily life, or what it feels like to carry adult expectations while still feeling unsure of herself. Those questions are not asked. The focus stays practical. Someone suggests more reminders. Someone else mentions flexible scheduling. These are offered as solutions. They address attendance, not exhaustion. Jemma agrees. Agreement is treated as sufficient protection.

The plan remains unchanged. It absorbs the slips without shifting shape. This reassures everyone that things are under control. It also delays deeper questions.

Jemma begins to feel she is being measured against an idea of motherhood she has not yet reached. She listens to advice about routines and preparation while still struggling to organise her own days. The gap widens quietly.

Professionals repeat advice she has already heard. The repetition suggests something is not sticking. She nods again. She does not say that remembering is difficult when nothing in her life is settled.

The tiredness deepens. It affects her concentration, her patience. She becomes quieter in appointments. This is noted as low mood or fatigue related to pregnancy. The explanation is enough. It does not lead further. When slips are discussed, they are framed as understandable. This framing is kind. It also prevents escalation. Understanding becomes a reason to wait.

Jemma recognises the kindness and its limits. It depends on her continuing to appear cooperative. She keeps smiling when she can. Apologising when she must.

The notes continue. Variable engagement. Some support required. Flexible phrases that stretch to cover what is happening. They allow concern without demanding change. No one asks what it feels like to sit in these rooms knowing every answer is recorded. No one asks what it feels like to be expected to perform readiness while still feeling like a child. These questions do not fit easily into forms.

Each slip passes without consequence. Together, they begin to gather. No one names that yet. Naming it would require a shift.

Jemma continues to move through appointments carefully. The system moves with her. Adjusting slightly. Not stopping. The story holds, though it is starting to strain.

Missed visits. Alcohol mentioned quietly. Excuses logged. Each absorbed. The narrative continues, even as the ground beneath it shifts. For now, the language stays gentle. Variable engagement. Some support required. These phrases keep everything in place. They allow everyone to believe things remain manageable.

Jemma leaves appointments with the same mix of relief and fatigue. Relief that nothing has escalated. Fatigue from holding it together. The slips do not yet change how she is seen. They are treated as temporary, not cumulative. The pattern remains unnamed. She keeps going. Keeps trying to be agreeable. Keeps answering carefully. Keeps attending enough to stay within tolerance.

No one asks what it costs her.

No one asks how it feels.

The slips remain what they are allowed to be.

Small.

Isolated.

Manageable.

The Birth

The hospital is organised around routine. Movement flows from one task to the next without pause. Corridors are clean. The lighting is bright enough to work under at any hour. Staff move with familiarity, speaking in shorthand, adjusting equipment, checking charts. Nothing suggests this moment is singular. It is one of many, folded into a shift.

The record begins with time. The hour is noted precisely. Then the date. Then the weight. Numbers are entered carefully because numbers matter. They are reliable. They allow comparison. Apgar scores follow, recorded without comment because they fall within the expected range. Satisfactory. No resuscitation required. No complications during delivery. These phrases carry reassurance. Nothing unexpected has happened.

There is no crisis. No emergency call. No shift in tone. The birth proceeds according to protocol. Pain is managed. Instructions are followed. Staff remain calm because there is no reason not to be. The calm is procedural, not emotional. It belongs to the environment.

Jemma is present throughout. This is noted indirectly, through the absence of concern. She is described through observation rather than narrative. She follows instructions. Answers questions when asked. Does not shout or panic. Does not resist. These behaviours are recorded as positives.

Someone notes that she appears calm. The observation is written down. Calmness is valued. It suggests cooperation. Stability. No one records how long she has been awake, or how little she has slept in the weeks before. No one records how fear might sit quietly rather than loudly. Those details do not fit the form.

She is asked standard questions. She answers them. Some responses come quickly. Others take a moment longer. This is not remarked on. Fatigue is assumed. Exhaustion is expected. There is no need to look further.

The delivery is handled efficiently. Instructions are clear. Jemma follows them. There is no note of distress. No note of dissociation. No space to record whether she feels present in her body or separate from it. The form does not ask.

Declan is delivered and taken briefly for checks. His cry is noted. His colour assessed. He is returned. The process continues. There is no extended commentary. The outcome meets expectation.

Staff speak in reassuring tones. Well done. He looks good. Everything went smoothly. The phrases are familiar. They are meant to comfort. They also signal closure. The difficult part is over. The system moves on.

Jemma listens. She nods. She does not ask many questions. This is read as trust. It is also fatigue. It is also habit. No one distinguishes between them.

Forms are completed. Times recorded. Signatures added. The documentation is thorough in the ways it needs to be. It confirms that procedures were followed and outcomes achieved.

There is a brief period of observation. Vital signs are checked. Declan is monitored. Jemma is monitored. Everything remains within acceptable limits. There is no reason to extend the stay. This is a success.

The language reflects that. Straightforward delivery. Healthy baby boy. Mother coping well. These phrases close the narrative. They suggest completion.

Jemma is described as appropriate. Cooperative. Calm. The words appear without elaboration. They do not require it. They serve their purpose.

No one writes about fear. That would require context. It would require questions. It would complicate the story. Its absence keeps the record uncomplicated.

No one writes about dissociation. That would require noticing something subtle, asking how she feels, not just how she is coping. The difference is not captured.

No one writes about exhaustion beyond what is expected. The kind that comes from a life already stretched thin has no place to be recorded. Only physical recovery is tracked.

The birth is considered complete once Jemma and Declan are stable. The next steps follow. Feeding. Postnatal checks. Discharge planning. The focus moves forward immediately.

Jemma is given information, verbally and in print. Leaflets are placed nearby. She is told who will see her next, and when. She listens. Takes in what she can. The rest blurs.

She holds Declan briefly. The interaction is observed. It is considered adequate. There is no cause for concern. The moment is not lingered on. It is enough that nothing adverse is seen.

The ward continues around her. Other births. Other babies. Staff moving in and out. Her experience is not separate. It is part of the flow.

When she is discharged, it is at the expected time. She meets the criteria. She is given instructions and contact numbers. She signs where required. The discharge is logged.

The file closes the event neatly. Birth completed. Mother and baby discharged. Follow-up arranged. The narrative does not extend beyond this point. There is no space to reflect on what it means beyond the clinical facts.

For the system, the birth is a success. A baby delivered alive. No complications. Protocol followed. Resources used as intended. The outcome meets expectation.

Relief sits quietly in the margins. Not emotional relief. Procedural relief. Another event concluded without incident.

Jemma leaves the hospital with Declan and a set of instructions. She carries him carefully. She looks as she is expected to look. No alarm is raised. No concern escalated.

The hospital returns to routine. Another bed prepared. Another patient arrives. Staff move on.

The birth becomes an entry in a file. It is complete. Contained. It does not require revisiting.

What is not written does not disrupt this. Fear. Disorientation. The weight of responsibility settling suddenly and heavily. These sit outside the record. They do not challenge the assessment of success.

The system has done what it needed to do. A baby delivered safely. A mother monitored. Both discharged according to guidelines.

The event is finished.

For Jemma, it does not end there. But the record does not follow her beyond the door. It closes with confidence. The outcome has been achieved. The box is ticked.

The birth is logged as uncomplicated. That becomes the defining feature. Everything else falls away.

This is how the event is held.

Cleanly.

Efficiently.

Without residue.

"Mother reports feeding issues. Baby observed to be settled. No immediate concerns."

Health visitor note, NHS records, 1982

Basic Neglect

The concerns do not arrive as alarms. They surface gradually, almost politely, at the edges of routine checks and brief conversations. Someone asks how feeding is going. The answer is not reassuring, but not alarming either. Declan is feeding. Just not regularly. Sometimes he finishes a bottle. Sometimes he does not. Sometimes he settles. Sometimes he cries for long stretches. The details are shared without urgency and received the same way.

Missed feeds are first described as irregularity rather than absence. A bottle delayed. Another skipped because he fell asleep. Diluted formula is not named at the outset. It is described as stretching. Making it last. Adjusting ratios because he seems sick afterwards. The language remains careful. No one says hungry. Hunger would interrupt the flow.

In the notes, Declan becomes unsettled. Difficult to soothe. Awake for long periods. Crying more than expected. These are familiar descriptions. They appear in many files. They are read as temperament rather than consequence.

Jemma offers explanations when asked. She is tired. She has not been sleeping. He refuses the bottle some days. She has tried different teats. Tried feeding more often. The tiredness shows. She looks drawn. Speaks more slowly than before. It is taken as normal. New mothers are tired. No distinction is made between tiredness that follows disruption and tiredness that follows not enough.

Advice is given. Feed little and often. Establish a routine. Keep a record. Prepare the formula correctly. The tone remains calm. The concern is noted, then deferred. Feeding will be reviewed at the next visit. Another follow-up is scheduled. It creates the sense that something is being done.

Declan's weight is checked. It is lower than expected, but not dramatically so. The chart dips slightly. This is described as something to watch rather than something to act on.

The language continues to soften what is happening. Unsettled rather than underfed. Fussy rather than hungry. Difficult to soothe rather than distressed. Jemma listens. Repeats the advice back. Says she understands. Says she will try. Her agreement is read as engagement. It reassures the room.

No one asks how long Declan goes between feeds on his worst days. No one asks what the nights are like when he cries.

When he cries during a visit, it is attributed to wind. To colic. The visits are brief. Observations are made in moments. Each one incomplete. Over time, he becomes a difficult feeder. Hard to settle. The focus shifts to his temperament. A difficult baby requires patience. A hungry baby would require action.

Follow-up is scheduled again. Another check. Another opportunity for improvement. When his weight is checked again, it has not increased as hoped. The chart is reviewed. Variation is discussed. Growth spurts are mentioned. The notes emphasise advice given, not advice followed. Intention, not outcome.

Declan's experience remains indirect. His cries are heard, but translated into manageable terms.

There is no single moment when someone says this is not working. Concern rises slightly, then settles again. Jemma continues to attend. Continues to agree. Continues to try.

The words that would require immediate action are not used.

Instead, there is monitoring.

Follow-up.

Time stretches the problem. Each observation, taken alone, is not enough to force change.

Not fed is not written anywhere. Instead, softer words are chosen, the reality sidestepped by phrases that avoid naming the problem directly, ensuring the most urgent truth remains unsaid.

The language holds firm, maintaining a veneer that prevents uncomfortable truths from surfacing, even as underlying problems remain unaddressed and continue to accumulate.

This careful choice of words offers a shield for the adult, gently deflecting scrutiny and responsibility while ensuring their actions or omissions are never directly questioned or challenged.

In contrast, the child is left waiting, their needs postponed by these softened explanations, as the urgency of their discomfort is lost in the delays created by indirect language and ongoing monitoring.

Logged and Ignored

The pattern continues without interruption. It does not escalate in a way that demands immediate response. It simply persists.

At visits, someone notices that Declan has not been changed recently. The nappy is heavy, and there is a smell of urine that lingers even after he is lifted and cleaned. These observations are made quietly and written down briefly, often at the end of a note, as if they are secondary to the main purpose of the visit.

His skin shows irritation, redness around the thighs, a rash beginning to form. This is pointed out, and advice is given about barrier cream, about changing more frequently, about letting the skin dry properly. Jemma listens and agrees. She says she has been trying. She says he goes through nappies quickly and she struggles to keep up. The explanation is accepted because it fits the picture already forming of a young mother doing her best under strain.

No one treats this as urgent. Nappy rash is common. Babies smell sometimes. New parents make mistakes. These explanations are available, and they are used. Each one softens what is being seen.

The details remain in the margins of visits rather than at the centre. They are mentioned after weight and feeding have been discussed. They do not alter the tone of the conversation. They do not lead to escalation. They are folded into the wider narrative of inexperience.

Neglect is not the word anyone uses. The behaviour is framed as inconsistency, as difficulty adjusting, as something that will improve as Jemma becomes more confident. The assumption is that support will correct it.

Declan cries during some visits when his nappy is changed. His discomfort is visible. This is interpreted as sensitivity or dislike of handling. Babies protest being changed. The explanation is reasonable. It does not require further thought.

Advice is repeated. Change him more often. Use cream. Keep an eye on his skin. Jemma nods. Her agreement is taken as evidence that the issue is being addressed.

The visits are short. There is limited time to observe what happens between them. Each visit offers only a glimpse. That glimpse is enough to note concern, but not enough to force a conclusion.

There is always another visit planned. Review next week. Check again. See if there is improvement. The plan absorbs the concern. Time becomes the response.

Jemma leaves each visit with a sense that she has been noticed but not challenged. This is a relief. It also means that nothing changes materially. She returns to the same circumstances with the same limitations.

The smell appears again at another visit. The irritation persists. Each time, it is noted briefly and explained in the same terms. New parent. Learning. Needs more support.

The narrative of progress is preserved carefully. Jemma is still described as engaging. She is still attending some appointments. She is still receptive to advice. These positives outweigh the negatives in the written record.

Each individual sign is insufficient on its own to force action. Together, they form a picture that is slowly emerging, but no one stops long enough to assemble it.

Supplies are discussed once. Someone asks whether she has enough nappies. She says she does. The answer is accepted. There is no follow-up.

No one asks how often Declan is left unchanged overnight. No one asks what happens on days when she is too tired to manage. These questions would require answers that might disrupt the narrative.

The system continues to work as designed. It monitors, it advises, it schedules follow-up. It waits for change.

Declan's discomfort is seen, but it is interpreted through a lens that minimises urgency. His cries are heard but framed as ordinary. His smell is noticed but attributed to inexperience rather than neglect.

Another visit is booked. Another opportunity to do better. Another chance to show improvement.

Nothing yet is enough to interrupt the story the system is telling itself. The story is that this is manageable. That support will be effective. That patience is appropriate.

The pattern continues. Not changed often enough. Skin irritated. Smell noted. Advice given. Follow-up planned.

The language remains gentle. The response remains measured. The urgency does not arrive.

For now, the system moves forward, confident that improvement is coming. Declan remains within that confidence, waiting for change that has not yet begun.

Risk Unchallenged

Declan begins to be left with other people in a way that is mentioned casually at first, almost as background information rather than a change in circumstance. Jemma says she is popping out. She says she will be back soon. Sometimes she names who he is with. Sometimes she does not. Friends. Someone she knows from where she is staying. A woman who has helped before. The details shift from one conversation to the next, and no one pauses long enough to line them up.

At the start, the absences are short. An hour or two while she goes to the shop or meets someone. This is not unusual. New parents rely on others. The assumption is that Declan is being looked after by someone Jemma trusts, and that trust is taken at face value. No one asks how long she has known them or how well. No one asks whether they are sober or prepared. These questions feel intrusive. They are not asked.

As time goes on, the gaps stretch. An afternoon becomes an evening. An overnight stay becomes two nights. Jemma explains that plans changed. She needed help. She was exhausted. These explanations are plausible. They fit the narrative of a young mother struggling but supported by a network around her.

Declan is sometimes left with people whose names appear once in the file and then never again. Other times there is no name at all. He was with a friend. He was with someone she knows. The lack of specificity is not challenged. The assumption is that if there were a problem, it would have been raised.

Hours become days without anyone marking the transition. There is no clear line between babysitting and abandonment in the way it is discussed. Responsibility becomes blurred. It is not clear who agreed to what, or for how long. Each arrangement is treated as informal and temporary.

When someone asks how long Declan was left, the answers are vague. A couple of days. Just overnight. Not long. These answers are accepted because there is no immediate evidence of harm. Declan is alive. He is present at the next visit. The system tends to respond to what it sees.

The people he is left with are not assessed. There is no check on their suitability. No questions about their capacity to care for a baby. The assumption is that Jemma would not leave her child with someone unsafe. It is a generous assumption. It also shifts responsibility away from scrutiny.

Jemma trusts these people because she has to. She needs rest. She needs to go somewhere without a baby. She needs space. These needs are real, but they are not examined closely. They are framed as understandable rather than risky.

When Declan is returned to her care, he sometimes appears unsettled. This is noted. It is attributed to disruption in routine. Babies do not like change. The explanation fits. It does not prompt further inquiry.

There is no single moment when someone says this is too much. Each instance of being left is considered on its own. One night away is manageable. Two nights can be explained. A third is still within the bounds of flexibility. Accumulation does not announce itself clearly.

The file records these arrangements in passing. Left with friend overnight. Returned the following day. Staying with acquaintance. The language remains neutral. It does not signal concern.

Jemma does not describe these absences as leaving. She describes them as getting help, as needing a break, as sorting things out. The language she uses shapes how the information is received. Getting help sounds responsible. Leaving sounds careless. Help is assumed.

Declan's care during these periods is largely unknown. No one asks what he was fed. No one asks how often he was changed. No one asks how he slept. These details would be hard to verify and uncomfortable to pursue.

The system relies on the idea that care is continuous unless proven otherwise. Declan is seen periodically. If he is present and alive, continuity is assumed. The spaces in between visits remain unexamined.

Jemma continues to attend some appointments during this time. This reinforces the belief that she is engaged. Her attendance compensates for concern about her absences. It suggests that she is still functioning.

Responsibility for Declan becomes shared in a way that no one oversees. He moves between adults without a clear plan. Each person involved may believe the arrangement is short term. No one holds the whole picture.

When questions are asked, they are gentle. Who has been helping you. Have you had some support. These questions invite reassurance rather than detail. Jemma reassures them. She says she has people around her. This is accepted.

The idea that a baby might be left for days without consistent care is difficult to hold. It challenges assumptions about maternal instinct and responsibility. It is easier to assume that things are muddled rather than wrong.

Declan's routines become inconsistent. Feeding times change. Sleep is disrupted. This is noted indirectly. He is unsettled. He is difficult to settle. These descriptors continue to be used. They mask the cause.

Each instance of being left is treated as accidental or understandable. Jemma was overwhelmed. She needed a break. The person was happy to help. These explanations are reasonable in isolation.

No one connects the frequency of these absences to the earlier concerns about feeding and changing. Each issue is compartmentalised. This compartmentalisation prevents escalation.

The absence of a crisis allows patience to continue. There is no injury. No report of immediate harm. Declan does not arrive at visits with obvious signs of abuse. This reassures those involved.

Accumulation is harder to act on than crisis. It requires someone to stop and look back rather than forward. The system is oriented towards what comes next rather than what has been building.

Jemma senses that these arrangements are tolerated. She continues to rely on them. She does not hide them, but she does not elaborate either. She offers information as asked and no more.

There are moments when she leaves Declan with someone intending to return the same day and does not. Plans change. She stays longer than expected. She does not always inform the person caring for him what is happening. Communication breaks down. Responsibility blurs further.

The people caring for Declan may assume Jemma will be back soon. When she is not, they manage as best they can. They may not have supplies. They may not have instructions. These details are not recorded.

When Declan is returned to Jemma, there is relief. The arrangement has ended. The focus moves on. No one asks what it was like for him during that time.

Professionals continue to view Jemma as overwhelmed rather than negligent. This framing matters. It shapes responses. Overwhelm can be supported. Neglect requires action.

The language used in the file reflects this. Left with friend for support. Stayed with acquaintance while mother unwell. These phrases soften the reality of prolonged absence.

Declan becomes increasingly passed between carers. This movement is not tracked formally. There is no record of who he is with and for how long. Without this information, risk is difficult to assess.

The system relies on thresholds that are not quite met. Leaving a child for a night is not enough. Leaving them for two nights is still explainable. Even several days can be rationalised if there is someone else involved.

There is no single moment when someone decides this is dangerous. Instead, there is a slow normalisation. What would have raised concern earlier becomes familiar.

Jemma continues to present as cooperative. She does not appear defensive when asked about Declan's care. This reassures professionals. It suggests transparency.

The absence of alarm allows the pattern to continue. Each instance adds weight, but no one lifts the whole load.

Declan's experience remains fragmented. His care depends on whoever is available. His routines are shaped by circumstance rather than intention. This instability is not named.

The narrative of support and coping holds. Jemma is seen as someone doing her best with limited resources. Declan is seen as a difficult baby. These narratives reinforce each other.

Another visit is planned. Another opportunity to observe. Another chance to intervene later if needed. The focus on the future delays the present concern.

Accumulation continues. It remains harder to act on than crisis.

For now, the system moves forward, noting arrangements, accepting explanations, trusting that temporary situations will resolve themselves. Declan remains within this tolerance, moving between hands, waiting for someone to decide that what is happening is no longer acceptable.

No one has yet reached that point.

"Child presents with facial bruising. Mother's explanation accepted. Threshold not met. Consistent with NAI (non-accidental injury)."

Child protection meeting minutes, 1984

Declared Safe (Out of Area)

Jemma takes Declan to England again without telling anyone who might have questioned it. There is no meeting where the move is discussed and no phone call logged to say she is leaving the area. It does not appear as a decision in the file. It appears later, briefly, as information that surfaces after the fact. She is no longer in West Dunbartonshire. She is staying down south. Contact will be more difficult for a while.

No alert is triggered. No one contacts another local authority to say that a baby already discussed for concerns is now living elsewhere. There is no handover.

The absence is recorded and then set aside.

Jemma does not experience this as dramatic. There is no rush or visible crisis. She packs what she can. Clothes for Declan. Bottles. Formula. A few belongings that fit into bags she can carry. The journey itself is unremarkable. Trains. Motorways. Service stations. She has done this before.

This time she carries a baby with her. That is the difference. The weight is constant. The responsibility does not lift when she sits down. Declan cries during the journey. She feeds him when she can. She changes him when there is space. She manages in the way she has learned to manage, moment by moment, without a plan beyond getting where she is going.

In England, she stays with people she is not known to. Friends of friends. A man who has offered her a place to stay. Someone who says it will be easier there. The details are not fixed. She adjusts as needed. She does not register with a doctor. She does not contact health services. She does not know how to, and she does not want attention.

Back home, distance does what it always does. Once she is no longer physically present, scrutiny fades. Appointments are missed and marked as cancelled or postponed. Follow-up calls go unanswered. Messages are left and not returned. Eventually, the attempts reduce. The case does not close, but it quietens.

The behaviour that had already been fragile does not improve. Feeding remains inconsistent. Changing remains irregular. Declan is still unsettled. He cries for long periods. These things do not stop because Jemma has moved. They simply happen where no one sees them.

In England, there are no scheduled visits. No one weighs Declan. No one comments on his skin or his smell. No one asks how often he is fed. The absence of observation creates space. It allows problems to continue without challenge.

Jemma understands this, even if she does not put it into words. She has learned that being outside a boundary reduces attention. She has seen how absence works. She has lived it before.

The people she stays with do not ask many questions. They see a tired young woman with a baby and accept her explanation that things have been hard. They offer help when it suits them and withdraw it when it does not. There is no structure. There is no expectation of consistency.

Declan's care becomes more fragmented. Jemma leaves him with people while she sleeps or goes out. Sometimes she is gone for hours. Sometimes longer. The people caring for him may not know how to prepare formula properly. They may not change him often. They may not respond quickly when he cries. These details are not shared with anyone who might intervene.

There is no record of this period. No notes. No observations. No professional language to soften what is happening. It exists entirely outside the system that might have named it.

Jemma drinks more during this time. There is no one to moderate or advise. Alcohol becomes a way to cope. The impact on Declan is immediate but unmeasured. He feeds less regularly. He is handled less carefully. He is left alone more often.

The absence of witnesses changes the dynamic. There is no need to explain or reassure. There is no need to perform engagement. Jemma does not have to smile or apologise. She does not have to attend anything. The effort required to maintain the appearance of coping falls away.

What remains is the reality of caring for a baby without support, without stability, and without oversight. This reality is harsher than anything recorded previously. It does not escalate into a single dramatic incident. It wears down slowly.

Declan becomes quieter. He cries less loudly. He sleeps more fitfully. These changes would have been noted if anyone were watching. They are not.

The behaviour does not stop because the setting has changed. It becomes easier to continue because there is no interruption. There are no questions that force reflection. There are no visits that might prompt improvement.

The people around Jemma may notice that Declan seems withdrawn or hard to soothe, but they do not know what is normal for him. They assume babies are difficult. They assume Jemma knows what she is doing. Responsibility diffuses again.

Back in Scotland, the file records that Jemma is out of area. This fact explains everything and nothing at once. It explains why visits cannot happen. It also justifies waiting.

No one escalates the absence. No one asks whether a baby with existing concerns should be tracked across borders. The systems are not designed for this kind of movement. They rely on presence to function.

Time passes without intervention. Weeks blur. Declan's development continues without support. His weight changes. His skin heals and breaks down again. His feeding remains erratic. These changes are unseen.

Jemma does not contact services for help. She has learned that asking brings scrutiny she does not want. She manages as she can. When she cannot, she leaves Declan with someone else.

The environment in England is no safer than the one she left. It is simply less visible. The absence of oversight does not protect Declan. It removes the possibility of early intervention.

When Jemma eventually returns to Scotland, the time away will be treated as another gap. Questions may be asked, but lightly. What happened during that period will remain largely unknown. There will be no detailed account to assess.

This second move is not treated as significant by the system. It is another absence to be noted and then worked around. The lack of response reinforces what Jemma already understands. Distance reduces consequence.

For Declan, the move compounds instability. Care becomes less predictable. His needs are met inconsistently. There is no baseline of safety to return to.

What happens in England does not appear in the file. It does not inform later assessments in any meaningful way. The harm that occurs there is unrecorded and therefore uncounted.

The system resumes its interest only when Jemma and Declan come back into view. Until then, the absence holds.

This is how scrutiny is lost. Not through dramatic failure, but through ordinary boundaries and quiet decisions. A young woman leaves an area. A baby goes with her. No one follows.

The move is not panic. It is strategy shaped by experience. Jemma knows that geography changes how much attention she receives. She uses that knowledge. The consequences fall on Declan. His suffering does not stop. It simply happens where no one is watching.

By the time anyone sees him again, time will have passed. The opportunity for early interruption will be gone. The absence will have done its work.

England becomes another blank space in the record. What happened there will not be fully known. It will sit outside the official story, shaping Declan's body and responses without ever being named.

This is how harm continues.

Compliance Misread as Safety

When Declan comes back into view, the change is noticed almost immediately. He cries less. He makes less noise during visits. He does not protest as loudly when he is handled. These differences are remarked on with relief. Someone says he seems more settled. Someone else writes that he appears calmer than before.

The word improvement is not used directly. Settling. Adjustment. Coping better. These are familiar terms. They fit neatly into the existing narrative.

No one asks why the change has occurred. The absence of crying is taken at face value. Crying is difficult to manage. Silence reassures. During visits, Declan lies in his pram or on a mat. He looks around less. His movements are smaller. He does not reach out often. When he is picked up, he does not immediately stiffen or cry. This is interpreted as comfort.

Jemma appears less flustered during these visits. There is less need to apologise for his crying or explain why he will not settle. This is noted indirectly. The visits feel calmer. The room feels easier to manage.

Professionals speak about routines again. They say it looks like things are beginning to fall into place. A baby who cries less is assumed to be receiving what he needs. No one revisits the earlier concerns with the same urgency. Feeding and changing are still discussed, but the tone is lighter. The sense of pressure has eased. Quiet creates space for reassurance.

Declan's quiet is logged as behaviour. He is described as placid. Content. Calm during visits. These descriptors replace the earlier ones. Difficult to soothe no longer appears. Unsettled drops out of the notes.

Crying is a problem behaviour. Its absence is a solution. This logic is embedded deeply enough that it does not need to be stated.

Jemma does not comment on the change. She does not say whether Declan cries when no one is there. She does not describe nights or long stretches alone. She has learned that silence is rewarded. She does not interrupt that.

The visits become shorter again. There is less to manage. Less to discuss. A calm baby allows the conversation to move quickly through the checklist. Weight. Feeding. Sleep. Everything appears broadly acceptable.

Declan's body still carries tension. He startles occasionally at sudden movement. His eyes track slowly. These signs are subtle. They are easy to miss. They do not demand attention in the way crying does.

When he does cry briefly during a visit, it is quieter than before. The sound is less urgent. It fades quickly. This is seen as progress. Babies grow. They adapt. The explanation fits.

No one asks what it costs a baby to stop signalling distress. No one asks how often his needs go unmet before he stops asking. These questions do not fit into routine checks.

The calm is praised without curiosity. It is welcomed. It makes everyone's job easier. It suggests that earlier interventions have worked. It allows confidence to return.

Jemma receives positive feedback. He seems much better now. He looks more settled. She nods. She accepts the praise without comment. Praise reinforces the pattern.

The quiet changes how Declan is handled. People touch him more readily. They lift him without hesitation. They move him without bracing for protest. His lack of response is taken as acceptance.

No one asks whether he has learned that protest does not change outcomes. That lesson would be invisible unless someone was looking for it.

The system records improvement and moves on. There are still concerns, but they feel less pressing. The earlier tension eases. The case settles back into monitoring.

Declan's quiet follows him between visits. It shapes how he is seen by anyone who encounters him briefly. He is described as an easy baby. He does not demand much. This description circulates.

Jemma benefits from this perception. An easy baby draws less attention. It reduces scrutiny. It lowers the threshold for concern. Quiet protects her as well as the system.

There is no mechanism for registering what Declan is holding internally. His body adapts to inconsistency by lowering its expectations. This adaptation is not visible on a chart.

Silence is easier to manage than distress. Calm is easier to record than pain. When someone mentions how much quieter he is, it is with relief. The earlier crying had been difficult. It had raised questions. Quiet resolves those questions without requiring answers.

No one compares his current behaviour to what is developmentally expected. The comparison is to his own past distress. Less crying equals improvement. The logic is simple.

Jemma is no longer asked as many questions during visits. The urgency has faded. There is a sense that things are under control again.

Declan's cues become smaller. He signals discomfort less obviously. He waits longer. This waiting is not seen. Only the absence of noise is noticed.

The cost of quiet is borne entirely by his body. It absorbs the stress. It carries the memory of what happened when needs were unmet. This memory does not show up in routine assessments.

There is no language in the file for what is happening here. The closest available terms all point in the wrong direction. Settled. Calm. Coping.

These words close off inquiry. They suggest resolution. They discourage further questioning.

Jemma does not correct this interpretation. She has no reason to. Quiet makes everything simpler. It reduces conflict. It reduces attention. It allows life to continue with less interference.

Declan's stillness is mistaken for comfort. His silence is mistaken for contentment. This mistake is easy to make when visits are brief and context is missing.

The system prefers outcomes that look like improvement. Quiet fits that preference perfectly.

There is no crisis to respond to. There is no loud signal to interrupt the process. Accumulated harm recedes into the background. Declan lies quietly during another visit. Someone smiles and says he is doing well. The note reflects this.

The story continues.

Muted Warnings

Nothing changes abruptly. The case does not escalate or close. It settles.

The period after Declan's quiet is marked by fewer notes rather than different ones. There are still visits. Still phone calls. Still brief observations recorded in familiar language. What changes is the tone. Concern no longer presses forward. It spreads out.

Small inconsistencies are noticed and then left where they are. A missed feed mentioned casually. A delay in answering the door. A smell that lingers longer than expected. Each detail is registered and then placed back into context. Babies vary. Families cope differently. Nothing here is decisive.

The earlier unease has nowhere to attach itself. Declan is calm when seen. Jemma is cooperative. There is no single fact that demands follow-up. The absence of escalation becomes evidence in itself.

Questions are asked less directly now. How are things going becomes a greeting rather than an inquiry. Answers are received politely and not tested. The space for challenge narrows without anyone deciding that it should.

Professionals feel the shift, even if they do not articulate it. The visits feel easier. The room feels manageable. There is less tension about what might be uncovered. This relief matters. It influences how long people stay and what they look for while they are there.

Concerns that might once have prompted a second look are absorbed into the existing assessment. Declan has been unsettled before. He appears better now. Jemma has struggled before. She seems to be managing. Improvement does not need to be complete to be accepted.

There is still talk of risk, but it is abstract. Managed risk. Ongoing monitoring. These phrases remain available, but they do less work than they once did. They describe a posture rather than an action.

The case begins to feel familiar. Familiarity dulls urgency. It makes it easier to assume that what is seen is representative of what exists.

Warnings do not disappear. They soften. They lose their edges. They become background noise rather than signals. Without repetition or escalation, they do not travel.

What is missing is not information but connection. Details sit beside each other without being drawn together. The quiet that reassures also interrupts accumulation. Each visit starts fresh.

No one decides that the situation is safe. Safety simply stops being questioned with the same intensity.

The system does not withdraw. It remains present enough to feel responsible and distant enough to avoid confrontation. This balance is comfortable. It allows work to continue elsewhere without feeling negligent here.

Declan remains visible, but only in fragments. He is seen in moments that favour calm. What happens between those moments does not shape the record.

By the time contact begins to thin, the groundwork has already been laid. Reduced urgency feels justified. Less access feels explainable. The warnings have not vanished. They have been muted.

Nothing dramatic has happened. The days pass without incident, and the quiet persists. There are no crises to mark the timeline, no urgent events to force a reckoning. The subtle shifts go unnoticed, woven into the ordinary.

That is the point. It is the absence of drama that shapes the story. The lack of obvious change allows everything else to slip quietly into place. What matters is not what erupts, but what settles without comment.

The case moves forward on the strength of what is not demanded. Quiet holds. Oversight loosens. The space between visits widens without being named.

What comes next will feel like drift, but the direction has already been set.

Closed Doors

The visits begin to thin out without anyone naming it as a change. At first it is a reschedule here, a cancellation there. A health visitor who cannot make it this week. A worker covering sickness. The gaps are explained individually and accepted easily. No one marks the point where regular contact becomes intermittent.

Professionals change. One leaves the post. Another takes over temporarily. Notes are read quickly before visits. Context is absorbed in summary rather than detail. Each new person arrives with partial knowledge and limited time. They see what is in front of them and what has been written most recently. Older concerns sit further back in the file and carry less weight.

Information thins as it passes between people. What was once discussed becomes assumed. What was once noted becomes background. Each person holds a slice of the situation, but no one is positioned to hold it all at once. The picture fragments without anyone deciding that it should.

The home becomes harder to access. Appointments are missed more often now. Sometimes no one answers the door. Sometimes Jemma texts afterwards to say she had been out or that Declan was asleep and she did not hear the knock. These explanations are accepted. They sound ordinary. They do not suggest intent.

When visits do happen, they are shorter. There is less to discuss. Declan remains quiet. Jemma remains polite. The atmosphere feels contained. The absence of immediate concern makes it easier to move quickly through the checklist and leave.

Missed appointments are logged. Follow-up is attempted. Messages are left. The effort tapers when responses are slow. This is not abandonment. It is adjustment. The system adapts to what it encounters.

Expectations lower gradually. Where there was once an assumption of regular contact, there is now an understanding that access is difficult. Where there was once a push to see inside the home, there is now reliance on brief encounters and self-report. This shift is rarely discussed. It happens through practice.

The language in the file changes subtly. Phrases like unable to gain access appear. Contact attempted. Family unavailable. These entries describe facts without assigning meaning. They protect the relationship by avoiding confrontation.

Jemma learns that missed appointments carry few immediate consequences. She does not have to argue or refuse. Absence achieves the same outcome without conflict. She does not frame this as resistance. It is simply easier some days to stay away.

Declan is seen less often. When he is seen, he appears calm. His quiet continues to reassure. There is little that demands urgent attention during these brief windows. The absence of visible crisis allows the reduction in contact to feel justified.

Professionals speak about managing risk rather than understanding it. This shift is reflected in the way concerns are framed. The aim becomes making sure nothing overtly dangerous happens rather than exploring why things are as they are. Containment replaces curiosity.

Plans are adjusted to reflect reality. Visits will be attempted rather than scheduled. Phone contact will be used instead. This flexibility is described as responsive practice. It also reduces oversight.

Each professional involved works within their own constraints. Caseloads are heavy. Time is limited. Decisions are shaped by what feels manageable. A family that is quiet and intermittently available moves lower on the list.

The absence of clear escalation points makes it difficult to justify increased intervention. There is no new injury. No dramatic disclosure. No single event that forces action. The concerns that exist are cumulative, but cumulative concern requires time and attention to assemble.

No one has that time.

The door remains closed more often than open. When it does open, it is briefly and on Jemma's terms. This control over access is not challenged directly. It is treated as circumstance rather than choice.

Declan's routines remain opaque. Feeding and changing are discussed less because there is less opportunity to observe. Questions are asked, but answers are brief. Without contradiction, they are accepted.

The system continues to adapt by narrowing its focus. Safety is defined minimally. As long as Declan is alive, presentable and free from visible injury, the threshold for concern is not met. This definition is never written down, but it operates quietly.

Containment becomes the goal. Keeping the situation within known bounds. Avoiding escalation. Maintaining a line of sight, however thin. Understanding would require deeper engagement, and deeper engagement feels difficult to justify without clearer evidence.

Professionals change again. Another handover. Another set of notes skimmed. The same phrases recur. Variable engagement. Difficult to access. No immediate concerns observed. These phrases carry the case forward without altering it.

Jemma senses that the pressure has eased. Fewer visits mean fewer questions. Fewer questions mean less effort. She does not read this as safety. She reads it as space.

Declan remains quiet. His behaviour continues to work in everyone's favour except his own. There is little to react to. Silence fills the gaps left by reduced contact.

In meetings, concerns are raised, though tempered quickly. Access has been challenging. The family has been hard to pin down. The baby appears settled when seen. These points balance out the unease. The decision is usually to continue as is.

Risk management replaces understanding because it is easier to document. Risk can be scored. Understanding cannot.

The system does not withdraw entirely. It hovers. It checks in occasionally. It waits for something to happen that would clarify what to do next. Waiting becomes a strategy.

No one says that the doors are closed. They say access is limited. The difference matters. Closed suggests intention. Limited suggests difficulty.

The outcome is the same.

Declan's life continues largely unseen. The spaces between visits grow longer. What happens there is unknown. The system accepts this unknown because it does not yet demand response.

Containment holds until it does not. For now, it holds.

The case remains open. The door remains mostly shut. The picture remains incomplete.

This is how oversight thins. Quietly. Gradually. Through adaptation rather than decision.

No one believes they are doing nothing. Everyone believes they are doing what is possible. The gap between those beliefs and Declan's reality continues to widen.

The doors stay closed.

Parental Risk

Alcohol comes back into the file without ceremony. It does not arrive as a new concern. It reappears as something already known, already discussed, already contextualised. Someone asks how things are going and Jemma says she has been drinking a bit. Another note mentions that alcohol use remains an issue. The language is careful and familiar. It does not escalate.

Sometimes the reference is indirect. There is a note about tiredness that feels more than expected. There is a comment about late nights. There is a mention of people coming and going from the flat. The implication sits there without being drawn out. Drugs appear at the edges in the same way. A passing reference to cannabis. A concern raised by a neighbour and left there. Nothing concrete enough to act on.

These details are logged as lifestyle issues. The phrase appears more than once. Lifestyle suggests choice. It suggests autonomy. It suggests something that can be addressed with advice rather than intervention.

Alcohol and drugs are placed firmly in the adult category. They belong to Jemma rather than to Declan.

The impact on Declan is not explored directly. There is no line drawn between substance use and feeding. No link made between intoxication and missed changes. No discussion of what happens when a baby wakes and the adult caring for him is impaired. These connections remain theoretical and therefore optional.

Risk is separated from consequence. It is acknowledged that alcohol use exists. It is acknowledged that drug use may exist. Without visible harm, these remain abstract risks. Abstract risks are easier to hold at a distance.

When alcohol is mentioned, the conversation returns quickly to advice. Cut down. Avoid drinking when caring for the baby. Make sure someone else is present if you have been drinking. These instructions are delivered calmly. Jemma agrees. Agreement is noted.

No one asks how often someone else is actually present. No one asks who that person might be. The assumption is that safeguards are in place because they have been spoken about.

Drugs are even more peripheral. A comment in the file. A question asked and answered briefly. Jemma denies using anything regularly. This denial is accepted because there is no evidence to contradict it. The issue is parked.

The system requires proof to act. Proof of harm. Proof of neglect that can be attributed clearly. Proof of intoxication during a visit. None of this is available. The visits are too brief. The access is too limited. The behaviour is too contained.

Declan remains quiet during the visits that do happen. His calm undermines concern. A baby who appears settled does not align with the idea of significant harm. This disconnect matters.

When professionals discuss risk, they do so in measured terms. Alcohol use may increase risk. Drug use may impact capacity. These statements remain hypothetical. They do not translate into action without a trigger.

Jemma's substance use is framed as coping rather than recklessness. She is overwhelmed. She lacks support. She is young. These explanations soften judgement. They also delay intervention.

There is an unspoken hierarchy at work. Substance use without visible injury sits lower than physical harm. As long as Declan is free from injury or acute illness, the threshold is not crossed.

The separation between adult behaviour and child experience is maintained carefully. Jemma drinks. Declan appears fine when seen. These two statements sit side by side without friction in the record.

No one asks whether Declan is ever left alone while Jemma drinks. No one asks whether he is held safely. No one asks whether feeds are missed during those periods. These questions would require answers that might force a response.

When concerns are raised in meetings, they are balanced quickly. Yes, there is alcohol use. Yes, there may be drug use. But engagement has been variable but acceptable. The baby appears settled. Access has been difficult, but when seen there are no immediate concerns. The balancing act holds.

Substance use becomes another background factor rather than a focal point. It joins housing instability and missed appointments as part of the wider picture without reshaping it.

Jemma senses that this is an area where honesty could be dangerous. She does not disclose more than she has to. She answers questions briefly. She does not volunteer details. This is read as cooperation rather than evasion.

The system does not push. Pushing would require capacity and justification. It would also risk losing the limited contact that remains. Maintaining some contact feels preferable to losing it entirely.

The file continues to note alcohol use in the same way over time. Remains an issue. Ongoing concern. To be monitored. Monitoring becomes the response. Drugs remain at the edges. Mentioned and then dropped. Without confirmation, they are treated as possibility rather than fact. Possibility does not demand action.

Declan's day-to-day life during periods of substance use remains unseen. The nights. The long afternoons. The times when Jemma is less present. These are not captured.

The system relies on snapshots. In the snapshots, Declan is quiet. He is clothed. He is alive. The snapshot contradicts the idea of immediate danger.

Risk assessments are completed. Boxes are ticked. Substance misuse is marked. The overall risk level remains manageable. This assessment holds within its own logic. It is simply incomplete.

No one writes about cumulative impact. About what repeated exposure to inconsistency does to a baby. About how impaired care shapes development. These concepts are harder to evidence and harder to act on.

Jemma continues to drink. Sometimes more. Sometimes less. There is no clear trajectory. This variability fits the category of lifestyle rather than addiction. The distinction matters.

Support is offered in principle. Information about services. Suggestions of referral. Jemma does not take these up. This is noted but not pursued. Engagement with substance services remains optional until thresholds change.

The focus remains on what can be proven. Without proof of harm, action feels unjustified. The system waits.

Declan's needs remain secondary to this evidentiary threshold. His experience does not have to be named as long as it cannot be demonstrated conclusively.

The language in the file continues to separate adult choice from child outcome. Alcohol use recorded. Drug use suspected. No immediate impact observed. These phrases sit side by side.

Jemma benefits from this separation. It allows her behaviour to be contextualised without consequence. It allows the case to remain at the level of monitoring. The system tells itself that it cannot act on what it cannot prove. This feels responsible. It avoids overreach. It also avoids early intervention.

Substances remain present. They shape the environment. They affect responsiveness. They alter routines. None of this is captured directly. When Declan is next seen, he remains quiet. This quiet continues to neutralise concern. It is difficult to argue harm in the face of calm.

The file moves on. Alcohol use noted. To be reviewed. Drugs mentioned. No further action. What matters most is that nothing has happened that demands action in a way that can be defended later. The absence of proof becomes the deciding factor.

Risk is acknowledged but held at a distance. Consequence remains unexamined.

The system continues to manage rather than understand. It waits for something clearer. Something undeniable.

Until then, substances remain a background issue. Logged. Known. Contained. Declan lives inside that containment, unseen, while the record holds steady.

Known But Unchecked

A man becomes a fixture in the home in a way that is not announced. There is no formal introduction. His name appears in conversations once, then again, then stops being explained. At first he is referred to loosely. Someone Jemma is seeing. Someone staying over. Then the language shifts. He lives there now.

His name stays.

The file records him indirectly. There are notes about arguments. Raised voices overheard, tension building in the household. These are written as observations rather than conclusions. He is present, and that is enough to be noted.

When professionals attend, James is sometimes there. Sometimes he is not. When he is present, he sits or stands close to Jemma. He answers questions that are not directed at him. He corrects her casually. He finishes her sentences. These moments are small and easily dismissed. They are difficult to record without interpretation.

The atmosphere changes around him. This is not written down, but it is felt. Conversations tighten. Jemma's body shifts slightly when he enters a room. She stops speaking freely. Her sentences shorten. Where she once offered explanations, she now offers confirmations. Yes. No. That's right.

Her jokes become rehearsed. They land quickly and safely, as if tested in advance. She laughs at the right moments. The laughter does not linger. When silence falls, it stretches longer than before. She does not rush to fill it.

Fear is never written down. There is no checkbox for it. There is no space in the form to describe how the room feels when James moves or how Jemma watches him before she speaks. The absence of language allows the moment to pass without comment.

Declan responds before anyone else does. When doors open, his body stiffens. He freezes briefly, then looks up, searching faces before he moves or makes a sound. This behaviour is subtle. It does not register as distress. It is easy to miss unless someone is watching closely.

When James speaks loudly, Declan goes quiet. Not crying. Not protesting. Quiet. This is noticed but left alone. Babies are sensitive to noise. The explanation holds.

Jemma explains things more carefully now. Her words arrive polished. She anticipates questions before they are asked. She corrects herself mid-sentence. She avoids saying anything that might need clarification later. This carefulness is read as engagement.

When arguments are mentioned, they are framed as mutual. A disagreement. A row. Couples argue. Stress makes things harder. These explanations circulate easily. They soften what is happening without denying it outright.

There is no direct allegation of violence. There is no disclosure. Without these, the system has little to move on. It stays with what it can document.

James is not assessed. He is not the primary client. His presence is acknowledged but left unexplored. He exists at the edge of the file rather than its centre. This positioning matters.

Jemma becomes more guarded during visits. She checks James's reactions before answering. She defers to him subtly. When asked about routines or feeding, she looks at him briefly, then responds. This glance is quick. It is easy to overlook.

Professionals notice that Jemma seems different, but the difference is difficult to articulate. She is quieter. More controlled. These qualities are not inherently concerning. They can be read as coping.

The home feels less accessible. Appointments are missed more often when James is present. When visits do happen, they are tightly managed. Doors open only as long as necessary. Conversations stay on the surface.

Declan watches more than he plays. His movements are cautious. He tracks James's voice even when he is in another room. These behaviours are not dramatic. They are easy to explain away as temperament.

The file records that James is a partner. Sometimes it notes that he is involved. There is no deeper description. No assessment of his impact on Jemma or Declan. The system has no routine for capturing atmosphere.

When professionals speak to Jemma alone, James is often nearby. Within earshot. Within reach. Privacy is partial. Jemma adjusts accordingly. She does not disclose anything that could be overheard.

Fear fills the corners of the room, but corners do not appear on forms. The language available focuses on actions rather than dynamics. Without words for control or intimidation, the shift remains unnamed.

Declan's quiet deepens. He waits. He watches. He reaches out less often. This is not logged as a change. It aligns with the earlier narrative of settling.

Jemma's explanations become smoother. She anticipates concerns and neutralises them before they can grow. This skill protects her. It also protects James.

When concerns are discussed in meetings, James is mentioned briefly. He is part of the household now. The conversation moves on. The focus remains on Jemma's engagement and Declan's presentation.

The system looks for incidents. It does not find any that meet threshold. Arguments without injury do not trigger action. Control without evidence is difficult to prove.

James's name remains in the file. It appears and stays. His presence becomes normalised. What was once new becomes background. Jemma's body carries the shift even when the record does not. Her shoulders stay tense. Her voice stays level. She avoids spontaneity. These changes are not captured.

Declan freezes again when a door opens unexpectedly. He looks to James first, then to Jemma. This sequence is brief. It happens quickly. It is not written down.

The atmosphere knows what the file does not. It holds the tension that language cannot. It registers the unspoken rules that now govern the home. The baby knows too. He adapts in the only way available to him. He becomes still. He watches. He waits.

The file moves on because it cannot name what has shifted. Without language, there is no mechanism to respond.

James remains. The home feels smaller. Conversations become careful. Silence stretches.

Fear is not written. Control is not written. The change is not written in a way that carries weight.

But the change is there. It shapes every interaction. It alters how Jemma speaks and how Declan moves. The system continues to look for proof. The atmosphere continues to tell the story.

The baby listens.

Protection Denied

Money starts to appear and disappear in ways that do not line up with anything formal. There are weeks when Jemma seems able to buy food without hesitation and weeks when there is nothing. Benefits are mentioned occasionally, but the amounts do not explain the shifts. There is no regular wage. No payslip. No pattern that can be tracked easily.

Professionals notice the inconsistency without naming it directly. Someone asks how she is managing financially. Jemma gives a short answer. She is getting by. She has help. The help is not specified. The conversation moves on.

At first, the concern appears as inference. There are comments about people visiting late at night. There are notes about unfamiliar men in the building. There is mention of James being out and other men being present. These observations are recorded separately. They are not connected.

Rumour reaches services indirectly. A neighbour says something. A health visitor hears something in passing. The information is incomplete and second-hand. It is treated cautiously. The language reflects that caution. Possible concerns. Unconfirmed information. To be aware of.

Sex work is not named at this stage. Naming it would require clarity. Clarity would require asking questions that might disrupt contact. The system hesitates.

Jemma does not volunteer information. When asked about money, she answers minimally. When asked about visitors, she shrugs and says people come and go. She does not appear embarrassed. She does not appear defensive. Her tone is matter of fact. This makes it harder to press.

Over time, the gaps become harder to explain away. There are periods when money is clearly available and periods when it is not. There are purchases that do not align with benefits. There are nights when Declan is present while unfamiliar men arrive and leave.

Eventually, someone uses more direct language. There is a question about whether Jemma is exchanging sex for money. The question is asked carefully. The tone is neutral. Jemma does not deny it outright. She looks away. She says she does what she needs to do.

The file adjusts. Sex work appears as a term, but cautiously. It is framed as survival. As vulnerability. As something Jemma is doing to manage her circumstances. The language remains careful. It avoids judgement.

The impact on Declan is not explored in detail. The concern is logged as an adult issue. A risk factor. Something that places Jemma at risk. The child is mentioned only indirectly as being present in the home.

There is no clear guidance for how to record what this means for a baby. The forms ask about supervision, about safety, about physical harm. They do not ask what a child witnesses or hears.

Declan exists alongside this economy. He is in the room while conversations happen around him. He hears voices change. He sees men he does not know enter and leave. He senses shifts in attention. These experiences are not captured.

When professionals visit, the house is quiet. There are no visitors then. The timing is managed. The visits are predictable. The activity happens outside of them. This separation protects the appearance of stability.

Jemma explains that Declan is asleep when she has people over. This is accepted. It is plausible. Babies sleep a lot. There is little reason to doubt her.

Questions about where Declan sleeps during these times, or who is responsible if she leaves the room, are left unasked. They would require answers that are difficult to hold.

The file records sex work as a concern for Jemma's safety. It notes the risk of exploitation, of violence, of substance use. These are real risks. They are addressed with offers of support. Information about services is given. Jemma does not take it up.

The child remains at the edge of this discussion. He is mentioned as being present, but the implications are not drawn out. The system lacks language for the kind of harm that comes from exposure rather than injury.

Money continues to come and go. The unpredictability affects routines. Food is plentiful one day and scarce the next. Declan's feeding remains inconsistent. This is noted elsewhere, but it is not connected here.

James's role in this economy is unclear. Sometimes he is present. Sometimes he is not. There are arguments about money. These are overheard. They are recorded as tension. The connection between control, money and sex is not made explicit.

Jemma becomes more guarded when the topic is raised. She answers questions carefully. She frames her actions as necessary. This framing is accepted because it aligns with the narrative of survival.

Professionals feel the limits of what they can do. Sex work is not illegal in itself. The presence of a child complicates things, but without clear evidence of harm, the threshold for action remains out of reach.

The file records that Declan is present in the home. It does not record what he experiences there. It cannot.

When concerns are discussed in meetings, they are balanced against other factors. Jemma is engaging intermittently. Declan appears settled when seen. Access to the home is limited. The picture remains incomplete. No further action is triggered.

Sex work remains a background concern rather than a focal point. It is acknowledged but contained. The system focuses on what it can prove rather than what it suspects.

Jemma continues because she needs to. There is no alternative presented that feels viable. The support offered does not address immediate needs. The money does.

Declan adapts. He remains quiet. He watches. He learns the rhythms of the house. These adaptations are not recorded. The file is not built to capture the atmosphere of a room when strangers arrive. It is not built to record the way a baby tracks movement or stills when voices change. It is not built for this kind of harm.

The language available focuses on risk factors and adult behaviour. It does not reach into lived experience. As a result, the concern remains abstract.

When professionals leave, the house returns to its other rhythms. Declan is there for all of it. He does not leave the room. He does not have a separate space. His presence is constant. What he sees is not written. What he hears is not written. What his body learns in those moments is not written.

The system continues to operate within its limits. Sex work is logged. The child is noted as present. No immediate action is taken. What cannot be proven does not trigger response. What cannot be named remains unaddressed.

Money comes. Money goes. Declan remains.

The exchange continues, largely unseen, held at the edge of the record, shaping a childhood that the file cannot describe.

The Referral

The referral does not arrive with urgency. It is not marked high risk or immediate. It comes through the usual channels, logged among others, written in language that has learned how to be careful. Concerns have been raised. Support may be required. There is nothing in the wording that forces a quick response or demands escalation. It asks to be considered rather than acted on.

The concern itself is familiar. A young mother. Inconsistent engagement. A baby who has been unsettled, then quiet. Periods out of area. Housing instability. Possible substance use. A partner in the home. None of these are new categories. None of them sit outside what the service already knows how to hold. The referral does not claim that something terrible has happened. It suggests that something might happen if nothing changes.

Social work re-enters the picture without tension. There is no sense of crisis driving the involvement. It is framed as support rather than intervention. This framing matters. It sets the tone for what follows.

The file is accessed and skimmed. There is too much of it to take in fully in the time available. Dates blur. Locations change. Names appear and disappear. Earlier concerns contradict later reassurances. The narrative does not move in a straight line. Trying to reconstruct it would take hours that no one has.

The decision is made, implicitly, to focus on the present. The present feels more stable than the past. The past is messy and complicated. The present can be addressed.

In the present, Jemma is back in the area. Declan is with her. There are no visible injuries. There is no immediate disclosure. The referral sits comfortably in the category of early intervention.

A visit is arranged. Not a statutory visit. A supportive one. The language around it is calm. Someone will come out to see how things are going. To talk about support. To see what might help.

Jemma agrees to the visit when she is contacted. She sounds polite on the phone. She does not refuse. She does not question the purpose. She says that is fine. Agreement is logged.

This agreement matters. It signals openness. It suggests cooperation. It makes everything that follows easier.

When the social worker arrives, the visit is brief. The house is quiet. Declan is present. He is clean enough. He is quiet. He watches rather than cries. The social worker notes that he appears settled.

Jemma answers questions in short, careful sentences. She describes things as difficult but manageable. She talks about being tired. About doing her best. About needing some help. She does not volunteer more than is asked.

The social worker listens. She nods. She offers advice. She talks about routines and support services. She asks if Jemma would be willing to engage with additional help. Jemma says yes.

This yes is written down. It is important. It becomes a reference point.

The visit ends without drama. There is no sense that anything has been uncovered. The social worker leaves with the impression of a family under strain but still within reach.

In supervision later, the case is discussed briefly. There is acknowledgement of complexity. There is also acknowledgement of limits. The service cannot go back in time. It can only work with what is happening now.

The referral is accepted at a low level. The aim is support. To keep an eye on things. To help Jemma stabilise.

Hope settles back in, quietly. Not hope in the sense of certainty, but hope that things might improve with the right input.

The language in the notes reflects this. Family agreeable to involvement. Mother keen to engage. No immediate safeguarding concerns identified at visit. No escalation is made. These phrases sit easily together.

There is recognition that the situation could deteriorate. This is acknowledged without emphasis. Contingencies are not discussed in detail. There is time.

The past is not interrogated. The time in England is mentioned but left unexplored. What happened there remains unknown. It is treated as a gap rather than a warning.

The earlier concerns about feeding, changing and being left with others are noted as historical. Declan's quiet now reassures those reading the file. He appears calmer than before. This supports the idea that things may be improving.

The presence of James is acknowledged. He is described as a partner. There is no assessment of his role beyond that. There is no evidence of violence. Without evidence, the concern remains theoretical.

Substance use is mentioned again. Alcohol remains an issue. Jemma is advised to reduce. She agrees. This agreement is noted.

The referral does what it is designed to do. It brings the family back into view without disrupting the surface of things. It offers help without challenging the narrative too directly.

The system responds as it is built to respond. It seeks to support rather than confront. It values engagement over consistency. It places weight on intention.

Jemma understands this instinctively. She knows that saying yes keeps things calm. She knows that engagement is safer than resistance. She has learned this over years of being assessed.

She continues to be careful with her words. She presents herself as willing. She accepts advice. She thanks the social worker for coming.

Declan remains quiet throughout the visit. He does not cry. He does not draw attention. This quiet does a lot of work. This kind of quiet is often mistaken for calm. It allows concern to stay low.

After the visit, the social worker writes up the notes. The tone is balanced. There are concerns, but also positives. The positives are easier to build action around.

Plans are discussed. Further visits. Possible referrals to parenting support. Nothing immediate. Nothing intrusive. The referral is not a turning point. It is a pause. A moment where the system checks in and decides to wait.

Hope settles back in because hope is easier to hold than fear. Fear would require decisions that feel heavy and irreversible.

The file grows by a few more pages. The story continues.

For Declan, the referral changes little in the short term. There is another adult in the house occasionally. Another set of eyes. But the rhythms of his days remain much the same.

For Jemma, the referral confirms what she already knows. As long as she engages, as long as nothing obvious happens, things will continue.

The system believes it has time. The referral has bought time.

The accumulation of what has already happened is not named. It is not drawn together. The referral stands alone, separate from the weight of what came before.

This separation allows optimism to return. It allows the belief that, with the right support, things might still work out. The goodwill is genuine. The intention is to manage risk carefully rather than ignore it.

The referral is closed to immediate action and opened to ongoing involvement. This feels like the right balance. Nothing is disrupted. Nothing is forced. The surface remains intact.

Hope settles in the space where caution might have been.

Child Protection

The threshold is crossed slowly, almost politely. There is no alarm. No urgent call. No sudden shift that anyone can point to later and say that was the moment. Instead there is a meeting. Then another. The referral is discussed again, this time with more people in the room. The language tightens without becoming sharp.

Concerns become risks. Support becomes monitoring. These words arrive quietly, but they change everything. They signal that the situation has moved from something that might improve on its own to something that needs watching. Watching feels like action without consequence. It allows everyone to remain calm.

Plans are written. They have headings. Timescales. Actions assigned to names around the table. There is reassurance in this structure. It gives the sense that things are being managed. Everyone agrees that improvement is possible. This agreement is not naïve. It is necessary. If improvement were not possible, different decisions would be required.

Those decisions feel too final.

Declan is discussed without being present. He exists in the room only as a series of descriptions. His body is reduced to words. Bruising noted. Weight concerns. Developmental delay. These phrases are read aloud and written down. Some responses are only visible if you know what to look for, and no one has to look at him while they say them.

The injuries are described clinically. Bruises to the back. Bruises behind the ears. Marks that are difficult to explain by accident. The tone remains measured. There is discussion about possible causes. Rolling. Handling. Rough play. Each explanation is considered and then set aside, but never fully rejected. The language leaves space.

Someone mentions that the location of the bruising is concerning. This is acknowledged. It is written down. It still does not force a conclusion.

There is discussion of feeding again. Reports that Declan has not been fed consistently. That there have been periods where he appears listless. That bottles have been missed. That weight gain has stalled. These are facts presented without drama. They are easier to hold this way.

Days without food is never said. The words are too heavy. Instead it is framed as inconsistent feeding. Missed feeds. Difficulty establishing routine. The effect is the same on paper. The weight of it is lighter.

The cupboard is mentioned. Not directly at first. Someone says Declan was found in a small enclosed space. That he had been left somewhere unsafe. The language circles the reality. Locked away. Restricted space. Inappropriate containment. These terms are used because they fit policy language.

The fridge is not mentioned immediately. When it is, it arrives carefully. A report that Declan was placed inside briefly. The word briefly does a lot of work. It limits the image. It reassures those listening that it was not prolonged. That it was not as bad as it could have been.

Everyone lets the words do the work so they do not have to picture the rest.

There is no description of the cold. The dark. The confusion of a baby placed somewhere that does not make sense. These details are not required for the meeting to proceed. They would make it harder to stay composed.

The injuries are real. The bruises on his back are noted again. Their shape. Their spread. The fact that they are not consistent with crawling or falling. The bruising behind his ears raises particular concern. This is mentioned by someone with clinical experience. Heads nod. The concern is shared. The explanation is considered but not resolved.

Still, the focus remains on what can be fixed.

Jemma is discussed in parallel. Her engagement. Her explanations. Her stress. Her relationship. The presence of James. The instability in the home. These factors are weighed carefully. There is an effort to understand rather than accuse.

Someone asks whether the injuries could have been caused by someone else in the home. The question hangs briefly, then is absorbed into the wider discussion of risk. There is no accusation attached to a name.

The plan expands. More visits. Closer monitoring. Parenting support. Safety planning. The belief is that increased oversight will reduce harm. That awareness will lead to change.

Declan's experiences are filtered through adult language. Bruises become injuries. Hunger becomes feeding difficulty. Confinement becomes inappropriate supervision. Each translation makes it easier to talk about. It also distances everyone from what it feels like.

The cupboard becomes a point of discussion. The fridge less so. It is acknowledged and then moved past. The focus shifts to preventing recurrence. Safety gates. Education. Advice. The assumption is that once told, the behaviour will stop.

There is discomfort in the room. It is controlled. People shift in their chairs. They look down at notes. They clear their throats. No one raises their voice. Professionalism holds.

Declan is not in the room to cry or resist or show what his body has learned. His silence makes the discussion easier. It allows abstraction.

Someone says that the injuries are significant enough to warrant child protection measures. This is agreed. The threshold has been met. The decision is made collectively, which spreads responsibility.

Child Protection is invoked. The words are spoken carefully. They carry weight. They also carry reassurance that the system is responding appropriately.

The plan is formalised. There are timescales now. Review dates. Clear expectations. The belief is that structure will produce safety. No immediate removal is pursued.

There is no question of how a baby learns to be quiet enough to survive being locked away. Or what it means for a child to stop crying because crying does not bring help. These questions are too difficult to answer.

The injuries are discussed again. Bruises heal. Skin recovers. Weight can be regained. These facts are comforting. They suggest reversibility.

What is harder to address is what does not heal as visibly. The way Declan freezes when doors close. The way he watches faces before making noise. These behaviours are noted elsewhere as settling. There is no pause to consider what it means that a child has already learned silence as survival. That he does not cry when frightened because it has never brought help.

In the meeting, this is left unspoken.

Jemma's explanations are considered. She is overwhelmed. She lacks support. She has made mistakes. These phrases are used because they allow room for improvement. They do not close the door.

There is an unspoken understanding that removing Declan would be a serious step. It would have consequences. It would require justification that no one is yet ready to give.

So the belief that improvement is possible is held tightly. It has to be. It is the only thing that allows the meeting to end without immediate removal.

Declan's bruises are described again before the meeting closes. The record will show that they were seen. That concern was expressed. That action was taken in the form of monitoring.

The cupboard and the fridge will be written down. They will be coded. They will sit in the file as incidents rather than experiences.

The meeting ends with agreement. Everyone signs off on the plan. There is a sense of gravity, but also of order. The system has done what it knows how to do.

Declan leaves the meeting as he entered it, as a subject rather than a person. His pain is real, but it is held at a distance.

Child Protection has begun. The language has shifted. The threshold has been crossed.

The belief that things can improve remains. It has to.

Outside the room, Declan continues to live in the atmosphere that produced the injuries being discussed. The plan has not yet reached him. It exists on paper.

The system moves forward, confident that it is responding appropriately. The cost of that confidence sits quietly with the child who is not in the room.

"Declan appears safe and bonded to foster carers. Recommendation: Maintain placement and review."

Social Work Report, Child Review 1984

Police

The police attend after an incident that cannot be explained away with careful language or deferred to the next visit. Someone has called. The call is logged. A unit is dispatched. There is a knock at the door that is different from the others. Louder. Firmer. It does not wait to be ignored.

They come in pairs. They look around before they sit. They ask where Declan is. He is brought into the room. He is small. He is quiet. He does not cry when he is passed from one adult to another. This is noted without being written down.

The officers look at him carefully. They do not rush. One of them crouches to be closer to his level. They ask how old he is. They ask how long he has been like this. They look at his back. They see the bruises that are still visible and the marks that are fading. They ask when they appeared. They ask how.

The questions are structured, but they circle. How did this happen? When did you first notice? Who was with him? Has he been seen by a doctor? Each question leads to another that edges closer without quite arriving.

Jemma answers carefully. Her words are calm. She has practised this. She says she does not know how he got the marks. She says he is clumsy. She says he bumps into things. She says he cries less now. She says she has been trying to follow advice.

James is present. He stands where he can see both officers. He answers some questions himself. He is confident. He does not appear nervous. He says he would never hurt a child. He says he helps out. He says people are overreacting.

The officers listen. They do not contradict him. They do not accuse. They take notes. They look again at Declan's back and ears. They look at the skin where the marks are. They do not touch more than necessary.

They ask about feeding. They ask when Declan last ate. Jemma answers. The answer is vague. The officer asks again, slightly differently. The answer shifts. This is noted.

They ask about where Declan sleeps. They ask whether he has ever been left alone. They ask whether he has ever been put somewhere for safety. The cupboard is mentioned. It is described as a mistake. The fridge is mentioned later. It is described as a joke that went wrong. The officers exchange a look. It is brief.

They ask whether Declan has been seen by medical staff. The answer is yes. They ask when. They ask what was said. Jemma answers in fragments. James fills in gaps. Together, the story sounds almost complete.

The officers explain that they need to establish what has happened. They explain that injuries to a baby are taken seriously. Their tone is measured. They are not unkind. They are careful not to promise anything.

They ask if there have been arguments in the home. James says couples argue. Jemma nods. The officer asks if arguments have ever become physical. Both deny it. The denial is firm.

They ask about alcohol. They ask about drugs. Jemma says she drinks sometimes. James says not around the baby. The officers note this.

They ask if Declan has ever been left with other people. Jemma says she has had help. The question is reframed. How long? With whom? The answers are incomplete. Names are given and then withdrawn. The officers note the inconsistency.

They ask to see the rest of the home. They look into rooms. They note the state of the kitchen. They look at where Declan sleeps. They do not open cupboards without permission. They do not look in the fridge.

Everything is documented. Times. Statements. Observations. The officers are thorough, but they are constrained by what they can prove. Atmosphere does not count. They need evidence that will stand.

They explain this gently. They say that without a clear account of how the injuries occurred, without witnesses, without medical confirmation that directly attributes cause, there are limits to what they can do.

They take photographs of the bruises. They ask for consent. It is given. The photographs are taken quickly. Declan does not react. This is noticed. It is not recorded as concern.

They explain the next steps. They will submit a report. They will liaise with social work. They will see if there is sufficient evidence to proceed further. They do not mention charges.

When they leave, they leave behind a quiet that feels heavier than before. The visit has not escalated into removal or arrest. Nothing dramatic has happened. This absence matters.

No charges are brought. There is not enough evidence. There rarely is at this point. The threshold for criminal action is not met. The bruises raise concern, but they cannot be tied conclusively to a specific act by a specific person beyond reasonable doubt. The explanations offered, while strained, cannot be disproven.

This absence carries weight. It is discussed later in meetings. The police attended. They did not charge. This fact reassures those around the table. It suggests that waiting is still appropriate. That caution remains justified.

The system breathes out.

The police report is factual. It lists injuries observed. It lists explanations given. It notes inconsistencies without drawing conclusions. It does not recommend immediate action beyond continued monitoring.

This document becomes another anchor point. It stabilises the narrative. If the police have not acted, then the threshold must not yet be crossed. This logic is rarely stated aloud, but it operates quietly.

Professionals refer back to the police involvement as evidence that things are being taken seriously. They say that the situation has been checked. That external scrutiny has occurred. This allows them to continue with the existing plan.

The absence of charges becomes a kind of permission. It suggests that nothing irreversible has happened. That intervention can remain measured. That there is still time.

The difference between criminal thresholds and child safety thresholds is rarely spoken aloud. It exists, but it is not held firmly enough to disrupt the comfort offered by the police decision.

Jemma feels the relief immediately. She does not show it. She remains composed. She thanks the officers for coming. She closes the door carefully after them.

James is louder after they leave. He paces. He talks about people sticking their noses in. He says they have nothing. This confidence reinforces the sense that the danger has passed.

Declan is quieter than ever. He does not cry during the visit. He does not cry after. He sits where he is placed. His stillness is read as calm.

The police involvement does not bring safety into the home. It brings a pause. It reassures the system. It does not change the dynamics that produced the injuries.

In later discussions, the police decision is used to temper concern. The bruises were investigated. No charges. The cupboard and fridge were mentioned, but there was no evidence of prolonged harm. The language does its work.

Waiting is framed as reasonable. Monitoring is framed as proportionate. There is caution about acting too soon, about overreacting.

The police have done their part. This belief settles in. It reduces pressure on everyone else.

The case remains open. The child protection plan remains in place. Nothing escalates. The absence of action becomes an action in itself. It shapes what happens next. It narrows the range of acceptable responses.

Declan's injuries begin to heal. Bruises fade. Skin changes colour. This visible recovery reinforces the belief that things are improving. It does not account for what has been learned underneath.

The officers do not return. There are no follow-up charges. There is no court. The incident recedes into the file as another entry.

Professionals talk about being guided by evidence. They say that without charges, they must proceed carefully. This sounds responsible. It feels defensible. Few ask what evidence would look like when harm is ongoing but fragmented. When injuries occur behind closed doors and explanations remain just plausible enough.

The police visit becomes something to point to. A reason to pause. A reason to breathe out. For Declan, nothing about the visit brings relief. The people who came and asked questions leave. The house remains the same.

The system holds the absence of charges as reassurance. It allows everyone to believe that waiting is not negligence. That caution is still appropriate. The police involvement closes a door as much as it opens one. It satisfies the need to act without forcing change.

This is how the moment passes. An incident that could not be ignored is attended, documented, and set aside. The file grows thicker. The sense of urgency eases.

The system breathes out.

The Plan

Created in a room where everyone knows how this works. There is a template. There are headings that appear in the same order every time. Risks. Protective factors. Actions. Timescales. Desired outcomes. The structure itself offers reassurance. It suggests control.

Reunification appears near the top. Sometimes it is written explicitly. Sometimes it is implied through the language used. Keeping the family together is framed as the goal. It is described as being in Declan's best interests. This assumption sits beneath everything that follows. It does not need to be argued for because it is familiar.

The harm that has already occurred is acknowledged, but it is framed carefully. Past incidents. Previous concerns. Historical issues. These words place distance between what happened and what is happening now. They suggest that the worst is behind them, even when there is no clear evidence that it is.

Risk is softened through phrasing. Managed. Addressed. Reduced. These words appear repeatedly. They create the impression that danger can be controlled through process. That oversight can stand in for safety.

The plan assumes cooperation. It assumes that if Jemma agrees to the actions, if she attends appointments, if she engages with services, then things will improve. This assumption is built into the structure of the document. Attendance is equated with change. Compliance is equated with safety.

Violence is not named directly. It appears instead as inappropriate handling, excessive discipline, unsafe practices. These phrases reduce severity without denying it. They make it easier to imagine that education and support will be sufficient.

Declan's injuries are referenced again, but briefly. Bruising noted previously. No new injuries observed. This absence becomes important. It suggests improvement. It allows the plan to lean towards reassurance.

There is discussion about James. His presence is acknowledged. He is included as someone who will need to engage. Expectations are set. He is asked to attend sessions. He is asked to cooperate with professionals. His agreement is assumed. There is no contingency written for refusal.

The plan outlines actions. Increased visits. Regular monitoring. Parenting support. Substance misuse services offered. Anger management suggested. Each action is assigned. Each action has a timescale. This distribution of responsibility creates the sense that everything is being addressed.

What is not addressed is what happens if these actions do not change behaviour. The plan rests on the belief that they will.

Language avoids absolutes. There are no deadlines for safety. There are review dates, but they are framed as opportunities to assess progress rather than points of decision. Removal is present only as an unspoken possibility.

Agreement around the table matters. Improvement is described as possible. This consensus allows the meeting to end without escalation. It allows everyone to leave feeling that the right thing has been done.

Declan is not in the room. He is discussed through reports and summaries. His bruises are described, not seen. His hunger is referenced as feeding issues. His confinement is discussed as supervision concerns. Distance makes discussion easier.

Someone reads aloud the section about Declan's needs. Safe care. Consistent feeding. Appropriate supervision. These statements are aspirational. They describe what should happen rather than what has been happening.

The plan assumes that awareness will lead to change. That, once named, behaviour will adjust. Harm is framed as accidental rather than patterned. Risk is broken down into components. Substance use. Domestic conflict. Inconsistent care. Each is given its own action. This fragmentation makes the whole appear manageable.

No one lists these risks together in a way that shows their combined weight. They remain separate. This prevents the full picture from becoming too stark.

Strengths are included. Jemma's engagement. Her willingness to accept support. Declan's quiet demeanour. These are written as balancing factors. They soften the assessment.

Quiet continues to reassure.

There is discussion about thresholds. About proportionality. About giving families a chance. These phrases are spoken aloud. They align with policy. They sound careful.

The plan prioritises keeping Declan at home while work is done. Safety is described as something that will be achieved through monitoring rather than immediate separation. This decision is framed as balanced.

Declan absorbs the cost of this balance. His safety is postponed in service of possibility. This is not written anywhere. It sits between the lines.

The plan is shared with Jemma. She reads it briefly. She signs it. Her signature carries more weight than its consistency.

She is told what is expected. Attend appointments. Allow access. Follow advice. Engage with support. These expectations are clear. They are also demanding.

No one asks how realistic they are given her circumstances. Capacity is assumed.

James is also asked to agree. He does. His agreement is noted. There is relief in the room.

The meeting ends with a sense of order. The plan exists. It can be referred to. It can be monitored. It can be reviewed. The structure contains anxiety.

Outside the room, nothing changes immediately. Declan returns to the same home. The same dynamics. The same adults.

The plan does not address the atmosphere in the house. It does not address fear. It does not address control. These things are difficult to measure and harder to act on. It focuses on what can be observed. Attendance. Cooperation. Compliance.

The language of the plan suggests progress before it has occurred. Reduced risk. Improved engagement. These phrases appear as goals, but they read like conclusions.

Declan's body remains the site where risk is absorbed. His responses. His quiet. His watchfulness. These are not part of the plan.

Review dates are set weeks away. Time is given.

In the meantime, professionals reassure themselves that they are acting proportionately. That they are following procedure. That they are not overreacting.

The plan allows everyone to believe that safety and reunification are compatible. That harm can be addressed without disruption.

This belief shapes what follows. Declan remains in place. The plan moves forward. Its coherence holds.

Its cost is carried quietly by the child it is meant to protect.

·

Instability Mistaken as Support

Contact increases after the plan is agreed. Visits are scheduled closer together. Phone calls happen more often. There is a sense that things are now active, that oversight has tightened. Each contact has a purpose. Each one produces notes.

Professionals arrive with checklists in mind. They look at Declan. They look at Jemma. They look for signs that the plan is working. Is the house clean enough? Is food visible? Has Declan been fed recently? Is Jemma sober? Is James present? Is everyone calm?

Each visit is observed, assessed, and quietly weighed against expectation. There is no literal scoring system written down, but the process functions as one. Small improvements are noted. Small failures are considered. The overall judgement shifts back and forth.

Jemma feels this immediately. She knows that every interaction matters now. She prepares for visits. She tidies. She times feeds. She keeps Declan awake so he will look alert. She manages herself carefully. She speaks in the language she knows is expected.

Pressure builds on her to demonstrate improvement. Not in words, but in presentation. The house needs to look calmer. Declan needs to appear settled. James needs to be cooperative or absent. These requirements are never listed explicitly, but they are understood.

Declan absorbs the other side of this pressure. He is expected to cope with increased handling, with being woken for visits, with being fed on schedule rather than when he signals. His cues are managed rather than followed.

During visits, Declan is quiet. He does not cry. He sits where he is placed. His body stays still in the chair or on the floor. This continues to work in his favour on paper. Calm baby during visit. Settled presentation. These phrases appear again. There is no space in the record for what the body learns.

Professionals note improvement. The house looks better. Jemma seems more organised. Declan appears well. These observations are accurate within the narrow window of the visit. They do not extend beyond it.

Between visits, the atmosphere tightens. James feels the scrutiny. He resents it. He talks about people interfering. His control increases. Jemma becomes quieter at home, more careful. She watches the clock in the days leading up to visits. She counts feeds. She keeps Declan awake longer than he wants to be so he will look alert when people arrive. The effort to keep things calm takes up most of her attention.

Violence fills the gaps the system does not occupy. Sometimes as rough handling. Sometimes as shouting close enough to be felt. Declan is present for all of it. He learns when to be still.

Little of this appears in the file. The file records what it sees. It sees scheduled visits. It sees polite conversation. It sees a quiet baby.

When visits do happen, they are brief. Professionals do not stay long enough to see what happens after they leave. They do not see James's expression change. They do not hear what is said once the door closes.

Jemma does not disclose what happens between visits. She knows that disclosure would escalate things she cannot control. She chooses silence.

The file reflects compliance. Jemma allows access. She follows advice when observed. This compliance is read as progress.

The plan requires improvement, and improvement must be demonstrated. This creates incentive to manage appearance rather than address harm. What is seen matters more than what persists.

Professionals record what is observable. Clean kitchen. Food present. No visible injuries. Calm interaction during visit. These observations accumulate and begin to outweigh earlier concerns.

There are discussions about whether things are improving. Some professionals feel reassured by what they see. Others feel uneasy. The unease is difficult to justify because the evidence supports progress.

Violence continues in the spaces the system does not see. It happens in increments. It happens off the record. It does not leave marks every time.

The file remains focused on milestones. Feeding improved. Weight stable. Engagement ongoing.

Each visit becomes a performance. Jemma performs stability. Declan performs calm. James performs cooperation. The professionals perform assessment. After each visit, the pressure eases briefly. Then it builds again as the next one approaches.

There is no single moment where removal is clearly justified. The harm is spread out. It happens between contacts. The system moves forward with the information it has.

The file does not follow it there.

When Evidence Challenges the File

The injury appears on a day that was meant to be routine. A visit that had been scheduled, moved once, then confirmed again. The door opens after a pause. Jemma looks tired. James is not there. Declan is brought into the room without fuss. He is quiet, as he has learned to be.

The mark is noticed almost immediately, though no one says so at first. It sits where accidents rarely land. Not a knee. Not a shin. Not a place that catches on furniture when a baby pulls himself up. It is on his torso, partly hidden by clothing. When he is lifted, when the fabric shifts, it shows itself.

Someone asks gently to take a look. Jemma hesitates, then nods. The clothing is moved aside. The room changes.

The bruise is deep. The colour is wrong. It spreads unevenly. The edges are not clean. It looks like pressure rather than impact.

The explanation that arrives a moment later fails to account for it.

It does not fit.

Jemma says he fell. She says he rolled awkwardly. She says he bumps into things. The words come quickly, already arranged. James is not there to correct her this time.

The professional listens. She looks again. She asks where Declan was when it happened. Jemma answers. The answer shifts slightly when the question is asked again, enough to suggest the story is being assembled rather than recalled.

Declan remains quiet while he is examined. He does not protest. His body stays still. His breathing changes slightly. This is noticed. It is not written down.

The bruise is measured. Its size is recorded. Its location is noted precisely. The tone remains calm. Calm keeps the visit contained.

A second injury is noticed then. Smaller. Fading. On the back of his arm. This one is harder to place. The explanation offered does not cover both.

The explanation does not fit. Further monitoring is arranged.

There is a pause.

The conversation slows.

The room becomes quieter.

The professional says the injury is concerning. She says it does not quite fit with the explanation given. She frames it as a question. Can you help me understand how this happened?

Jemma tries again. Her voice tightens. She looks at Declan while she speaks, then away. She says she is tired. She says she does not remember exactly. She says things have been hard.

There is discussion about what to do next. Some of it happens in the room. Some of it happens later, elsewhere. Options are considered.

Escalation is mentioned. The police have already been involved once. There were no charges. That fact sits in the background.

The professional explains that she will need to speak to her manager. She explains that further assessment may be required. She presents this as procedure. Jemma nods. She says she understands.

Declan is dressed again. He is placed down. He remains quiet. He watches.

After the visit, the injury is discussed again in rooms Declan will never enter. It is described carefully. Photographs are reviewed. The explanation is repeated.

The explanation is inadequate.

Someone says the injury is suspicious.

Someone else says suspicion is not proof.

Escalation without certainty can cause harm.

Waiting may also cause harm.

There is hesitation. Acting would be disruptive. It would require justification that will stand later. The earlier police decision is remembered.

No immediate escalation occurs.

The decision is made to monitor. To arrange another visit sooner. To see whether there are further injuries. This is written as proportionate.

The injury is recorded in detail. The language is accurate.

Declan returns to the same home with the same adults. The bruise is still there. It hurts when he is lifted. He does not cry.

Between visits, the bruise darkens and then begins to fade. Another appears before the first is gone. This one is smaller. Easier to account for. It is not seen.

When the next visit happens, the earlier bruise is lighter. It is still visible, but less striking. This softens concern.

The professional asks how things are going. Jemma says better. She says she has been trying harder. She says things are calmer. James smiles when he is mentioned.

Declan sits quietly. He does not draw attention to himself.

The injury that did not fit becomes one data point among many. It is balanced against other information.

There have been no new visible injuries since. Monitoring has increased.

The rationale is recorded. Proportionality. Lack of certainty. Need for further evidence.

The injury that did not fit lingers as a discomfort rather than a trigger.

The waiting continues.

No further action is taken at this stage. The file remains open, quietly. The decision sits, neither final nor forgotten, waiting for something to tilt the balance.

Escalation

Injuries do not slow down. They do not stabilise. They appear more often, though not in a way that announces itself at the time. Each incident arrives separately, spaced by days or weeks. Each is considered separately.

It is explained on its own terms.

Absorbed into the existing picture.

A bruise on his side. A mark on his shoulder. Redness that lingers longer than it should. Each one is noticed. Each one is described. Each one has an explanation attached to it. He fell. He rolled. He bumped into furniture. He is clumsy. Babies are clumsy. These explanations are familiar. Taken individually, they sound reasonable.

Professionals begin to note frequency. The plan remains in place. It comes up in meetings, not urgently, but as context. Someone says there have been several incidents recently. The word several sits where a number might have been. It allows concern without precision.

Each new incident increases concern, then settles again. The previous incident is referenced briefly and then replaced by the next. There is no list. There is no sequence. Without sequence, escalation is harder to hold.

The file grows thicker. The pattern does not.

Declan's body begins to show marks in different stages of healing. One bruise fading while another darkens. This is written down once, described carefully, then not returned to. The note exists, but it does not interrupt the plan.

Explanations become shorter. Jemma says she is unsure what happened. She says she was in another room. She says James was there. Then she says he was absent. The shifts are small. They do not trigger immediate challenge.

As scrutiny increases, James becomes more volatile. He resents the visits. He talks about people judging him. He says they are trying to take the baby. His anger has fewer places to go. At home, the pressure is constant. Jemma moves carefully. She tries to keep Declan quiet. She tries to anticipate James's moods. Sometimes she intervenes. Sometimes she cannot.

The police have already attended once. There were no charges. That outcome sits in the background. Visits continue. Nothing changes in a way that produces consequence. James learns this.

The incident that alters the tone arrives without warning, though it does not come from nowhere.

Declan is on the floor. He is playing with something small. He makes noise. Crying has not started. James is already angry. About money. About the visits. About things that cannot be resolved in that moment.

Jemma is in the room. She sees the movement before she understands it. James steps forward and brings his foot down hard on Declan's chest. He says it was an accident.

There is a pause where nothing happens.

The sound is dull. Declan's breath leaves him. He cannot cry because there is no air.

Then Declan gasps as his body tries to breathe again. His chest rises unevenly. He makes a sound that is not quite a cry. His body curls inward. His eyes are wide. Something has gone wrong.

Jemma picks him up. Her hands are shaking. She presses gently against his chest, and he cries, sharply, in pain. James is shouting now. He says he did not mean it. He says it was an accident. He says she made him angry. Redness spreads across Declan's chest. His breathing stays fast and shallow. He does not settle.

Time passes. Minutes. Longer. Declan cries when he is moved. Jemma watches his chest rise and fall. She counts breaths. Eventually, she seeks help. The details of how blur later. What matters is that Declan is seen by medical staff.

The injury is obvious. Bruising begins to form across his chest. There is tenderness. There is concern about internal injury. Questions are asked. Jemma answers carefully. She does not describe what happened. She says he fell. She says she is unsure.

The explanation fails to fit.

It is recorded.

It does not match the location or severity.

It remains on file.

The injury is logged. The chest injury is described in detail. There is mention of force. There is mention of risk. There is discussion about whether it could have been accidental. James is absent during the assessment. His absence is noted. It is not explored.

The professionals involved register the shift. The injury sits uneasily alongside the existing plan.

And yet, the response remains incremental.

There is discussion about escalation. About emergency measures. About removal. These words are spoken quietly, then set aside while other considerations are weighed.

The plan remains unchanged.

No immediate action is taken.

The police attendance returns to the conversation. No charges were brought. That fact carries weight. It limits what follows. The injury is folded into the existing concerns. It becomes another incident rather than the point that redefines everything.

The explanation is recorded. It does not convince.

Without disclosure, without a witness, action does not follow.

No one names what is happening directly. No one writes that this is abuse escalating. No one states that Declan is in immediate danger from a specific person.

The plan remains active. It assumes improvement is still possible. Declan is returned to Jemma's care after medical assessment. James remains in the home.

Nothing fundamental has changed.

Between visits, there are more incidents. Rough handling. Being grabbed too hard. Shoving. Declan cries more, then stops. His body shifts between protest and stillness.

New marks appear. Smaller ones. Easier to hide. Easier to explain.

The connections are not made. Professionals speak about unease in supervision. They say something is not right. They say the explanations are not adding up. Acting would require certainty they do not feel they have.

The file records escalation in fragments. Increased frequency of injuries. Inconsistent explanations. Heightened concern. These phrases appear, but they are dispersed.

No one writes the sentence that would change everything.

Declan's chest injury heals. The bruising fades. His body remains cautious. He flinches when adults move quickly. He guards his torso. He cries when lifted under the arms. Later, these behaviours are noted as sensitivity.

Jemma becomes more frantic. She tries to keep James away from Declan. She fails. She does not leave. The reasons do not enter the record. The system continues as it has been. It monitors. It plans. It waits.

Injuries appear more often. Explanations grow thinner. Each new incident raises concern, then settles. Escalation exists in hindsight, not in the moment. It is visible only when the pieces are lined up later. Until then, it remains distributed, defensible, and unnamed.

Declan's body carries the truth before the file does.

Pattern

The hospital visits begin to accumulate quietly. There is no single admission that feels decisive. No moment when someone says this is the one that changes everything. Instead there are different days, different wards, different clinicians, each seeing Declan briefly and then handing him back to the world he came from.

He arrives bundled in clothes that cover most of his body.

Sometimes he is crying. Sometimes he is silent.

Bruises. Tenderness. Marks.

The explanation adjusts to fit what is visible.

Seen repeatedly, but never all at once. The pattern is visible, but not held.

Clinicians document carefully. Location. Size. Colour. Stage of healing. They ask standard questions. How did this happen? When did you notice? Was he alone? The answers vary. Inconsistency is noted.

Suspicion appears in the notes. Non-accidental injury cannot be ruled out. Safeguarding concern raised. Young parents. Stress. Previous involvement. Social work already aware.

Treatment is given. Pain relief and advice. A follow-up is recommended. Tests rule out internal injury. This allows discharge. Ensure a safe environment. Monitor closely. Follow up with social work.

Declan returns home after each visit. Bruises fade. New ones appear later. The records are accurate. They are also isolated.

He arrives again. Clothes covering most of his body. Sometimes crying. Sometimes silent. Bruises. Tenderness. Marks. Explanations adjust. Each visit is treated in isolation.

Clinicians document carefully.

Location. Size. Colour. Stage of healing.

Standard questions.

Answers vary.

Inconsistency noted.

Suspicion appears. Non-accidental injury cannot be ruled out. Safeguarding concern raised. Context recorded. Treatment. Advice. Follow-up. Tests rule out internal injury. Discharge.

Declan returns home.

Declan is too young to tell anyone what happened. He cannot describe the sequence. He can only present with its aftermath.

The clinicians do not see his home. They do not see the atmosphere. They do not see how Jemma looks to James before answering. They see a quiet baby. Quiet lowers urgency.

There is a discussion at one visit about escalation. Notes are reviewed quickly. Yes, there are concerns. Yes, social work is involved. There is not enough to justify emergency action from hospital care.

No escalation is made.

The decision is defensible. It becomes another delay. Hospital attendances begin to cluster. Each visit sits in its own record. It takes time for someone to notice.

When it is noticed, it is in a meeting, not at the bedside. Someone says Declan has attended several times. The number is not specified. Bruising to chest. Bruising to back. Marks inconsistent with developmental stage.

No single document carries the whole story. The cupboard. The fridge. The shouting. The fear. These remain distributed across notes and memories.

Jemma begins to dread hospital visits, not because she fears for Declan's health, but because each one increases scrutiny. She becomes more careful about timing. She waits until injuries are less visible. She learns the rhythms.

Declan's injuries begin to overlap. One bruise has not fully healed before another appears. This is noted once as injuries at different stages of healing. The phrase is significant. It is brief.

The clinician moves on.

The system relies on accumulation to force action.

Accumulation requires connection.

When child protection meetings discuss hospital attendances, they do so from summaries. They hear that he has attended several times.

They hear that concerns have been raised. They also hear that he has been discharged each time.

Discharge functions as reassurance. If hospital staff were truly alarmed, they would have acted. This logic circulates quietly.

The pattern remains unnamed because it belongs to no single record. It is spread across systems that do not speak to each other easily.

Declan's body is the only place where the pattern is complete. It holds every impact. Every grab. Every moment when pain arrives without warning.

The clinicians see injuries. They do not see sequence. Without sequence, intent is harder to name.

The notes are careful. The language is professional. The concern is present. It is also contained.

Each visit ends the same way. Treatment. Advice. Discharge.

Declan leaves the hospital each time in his mother's arms. The automatic doors open and close behind him. The ward returns to routine.

Concern grows incrementally elsewhere.

It is discussed more often.

With each new entry, it becomes harder to dismiss the growing evidence of concern. The accumulation of incidents does not force an immediate decision, but it steadily increases the weight of responsibility.

Despite mounting concerns, the incidents continue to occur, each one adding to the narrative that is being assembled. As the situation unfolds, the file grows ever thicker, containing the details and documentation of each event.

Declan's body keeps the count.

Threshold

The shift does not happen all at once, but when it comes, it is unmistakable.

It is not a revelation. It is recognition catching up with what has already been recorded. Optimism, which has carried the case for months, can no longer hold the weight being placed on it. Too many injuries. Too many explanations that no longer align, even when read generously. Too many moments where the same questions are asked and the answers slide past each other without meeting.

The threshold is crossed not because something new has happened, but because accumulation is finally allowed to exist. Someone brings the documents together. Someone prints what had previously been read on screens. Hospital attendances are laid out in order. Dates are underlined. Photographs are reviewed again, this time without being separated by weeks or different professionals' notes. Entries that once sat in different sections of the file now sit beside each other.

Read in sequence rather than isolation, the record behaves differently.

The pattern is not new. It is newly held.

Bruises appear, fade, and reappear. Injuries occur in places that do not match Declan's developmental stage or reported activity. Explanations shift slightly from one incident to the next. None of this is new information. All of it has been documented. What is new is the decision to hold it together long enough to see what it says when it is not softened by time or context.

Someone points to a date and then another. Someone reads aloud a line from a clinic letter and then another from a home visit report. The language is careful, but the repetition becomes harder to ignore. It had been possible to ignore it. The same concerns, described in different professional dialects, recur. The effect is cumulative.

There is a pattern of harm that has been recorded without being named. The threshold is now considered met.

This time, the discussion in the room feels different. Chairs are pulled closer together. There is less informal conversation. People speak in shorter sentences. The phrases that once kept the case open now feel thin. Managed risk. Ongoing monitoring. Support in place. These words still exist, but they no longer reassure.

Someone says that the risk is no longer theoretical. Someone else says that the level of harm has increased. These statements are not challenged. No one offers a balancing comment. Agreement comes quickly. No alternative is proposed. Not because it is sudden, but because it has been waiting.

Urgency arrives late, but when it arrives, it is fully formed. It does not need to be argued into existence. It has been assembling quietly through repetition, through unease, through the accumulation of details that no longer sit comfortably apart.

The conversation turns practical. What needs to happen now. Who needs to be informed. What authority is required. The language shifts from possibility to sequence. There is less discussion about whether change is achievable and more discussion about immediate safety.

Someone asks whether there is any new information that would justify continued waiting. There is a pause. No one offers any.

Waiting is no longer defended.

That absence matters.

The earlier belief that cooperation could outweigh harm is released without ceremony. It had been maintained. Attendance and compliance are no longer treated as protective factors. They are acknowledged as behaviours that have existed alongside injury rather than preventing it.

There is acknowledgement in the room that waiting has carried a cost. This is not said directly. It does not appear in the minutes. It registers instead in the way people avoid eye contact for a moment before returning to the agenda. The recognition is quiet and procedural. Then the work continues.

Legal advice is sought promptly, ensuring compliance with procedural requirements and clarifying the necessary steps for safeguarding. The query is made with a sense of urgency, reflecting the shifting priorities in the room.

Senior managers are contacted immediately, their involvement marking a transition from deliberation to decisive action. Their guidance is requested as the situation moves beyond routine management, reinforcing the seriousness of the decision.

The language becomes firmer, shedding ambiguity. Instructions are delivered with clarity and certainty. The tone reflects the collective resolve in the room, as the conversation shifts from the exploration of options to the articulation of definite plans.

Immediate safeguarding measures are discussed without qualification.

Action is required.

There is no longer a need to frame them as contingency.

The plan that once prioritised reunification is no longer referenced. It is not formally closed at this point. It simply stops structuring the conversation. A different framework takes its place.

Someone says that Declan cannot remain in the home. The sentence is spoken plainly. It lands and stays. No one asks for it to be softened. No one suggests an alternative. The decision is made to act.

There is a brief silence. Then agreement.

From this point, the meeting moves with clarity. Tasks are assigned. Timelines are specified. Someone confirms who will lead the visit. Someone else confirms who will attend. There is discussion about minimising distress, about remaining calm, about explaining as much as possible without overwhelming.

These considerations are practical rather than emotional. They reflect the system's understanding of what removal requires when it becomes necessary.

There is fear in the room, but it does not derail the process. Fear of what has already happened. Fear of what may still be uncovered. Fear of scrutiny that will come later. These fears sharpen attention rather than delaying action.

The system, which has moved slowly for months, accelerates. Calls are made during the meeting rather than after it. Advice is confirmed rather than deferred. The pace changes because the decision has been made.

The justification is articulated clearly. Too many injuries. Inconsistent explanations. Escalating risk. Insufficient protective capacity. This language appears in the paperwork. It is designed to stand up to review.

Someone states explicitly that the earlier police decision does not prevent action now. This is said out loud. It breaks the hold that absence of charges has had on the case. The room acknowledges this collectively.

Declan's injuries are listed again. Bruising to the chest. Bruising to the back. Marks behind the ears. Injuries at different stages of healing. Periods of weight faltering. These are not new facts. Their arrangement is.

Environmental concerns are revisited. The cupboard. The fridge. This time, the language is direct. Inappropriate confinement. Unsafe practices. These phrases are no longer mitigated.

There is discussion of James. His behaviour. His presence in the home. His proximity to the injuries. His name is no longer separated from what has happened to Declan. The shift is evident without being overstated.

Jemma is discussed as well. Her vulnerability. Her fear. Her inability to prevent harm. These conversations are careful. They are uncomfortable. They are no longer postponed.

Compassion remains present, but its direction changes. Compassion is no longer framed as giving more time. It is framed as ending exposure to harm.

Plans are made for the visit itself. Who will speak first. Where Declan will be taken. What items will be gathered. How to manage the transition calmly. These details matter because the outcome is no longer in question.

Someone asks whether there is any safe alternative within the family. The answer is no. This is stated without debate.

The decision is documented and signed off at senior level. There is a visible shift in the room when this happens. The uncertainty that has dominated the case lifts slightly. Action, even when painful, brings a form of relief.

Notifications are prepared. Timelines narrow. The case that once moved in cycles now moves forward.

There is also reflection, though it remains internal. People think back over earlier decisions. Over the chances that were given. Over injuries that did not fit. These thoughts do not change what must happen now. They sit alongside the work.

The threshold has been crossed because it could no longer be avoided. The cost of waiting has become too clear. It could have been crossed earlier.

Those who will carry out the decision approach it with gravity. This is not routine, even if it is practised. Removing a child is always consequential.

Declan does not know that a threshold has been crossed. He does not know about meetings or documents. He knows only his body and the way it reacts to adults approaching.

Urgency does not reach him as reassurance. It reaches him as change. The language of proportionality no longer applies. Safety takes precedence. What was once framed as support becomes protection. The distinction matters.

By the time the visit is scheduled, there is no further monitoring period. No additional review. The case has moved into a different phase. The urgency feels late to those who have followed the file. It feels sudden to those living inside it. There is no celebration of the decision. There is only resolve. This is what must happen now. Once the threshold is crossed, there is no return to waiting.

Supervised Seeing

The visit is arranged for the morning. Not early enough to feel like an emergency, not late enough to suggest delay. A time that fits into working hours. A time that can be written down without explanation.

Two people arrive. They knock. They wait. When the door opens, they introduce themselves, even though they have been here before. Their voices are steady. Their expressions are neutral. This is not confrontation. It is procedure.

Jemma stands in the doorway with Declan on her hip. He is heavier than he looks because he does not adjust his body to be held. He stays rigid. His head is tucked into her shoulder. He does not look at the visitors.

James is not there. This has been noted in advance. His absence makes the visit easier to manage. No one mentions him.

They step inside. Shoes are left where they are told to leave them. Coats come off. There is a brief exchange about the weather. These small rituals matter. They keep the tone even.

They sit where there is space. They do not rush. One of them asks how things have been. The question is polite. It is also irrelevant. The answer does not change what is about to happen.

Jemma answers anyway. She says fine. She says she has been trying. Her voice is careful. She has learned that tone matters, even when words do not.

Declan shifts slightly. His hand grips the fabric of her top. His breathing is shallow. He is watching without lifting his head.

The social worker explains why they are there. The words are chosen carefully. There have been ongoing concerns. The level of risk is too high. They need to ensure Declan's safety. The explanation is delivered calmly, as if this were information rather than a decision.

Jemma listens. She does not interrupt. She nods once. Her face changes, but not dramatically. It tightens. She blinks slowly. She has known this was coming in some form, even if she did not know when.

They explain what will happen next. Declan will be taken into care today. He will be placed somewhere safe. There will be contact arrangements discussed later. The language avoids detail. It focuses on process.

No one says removal. No one says taken. They say placed. They say cared for. They say temporarily. These words are meant to soften what is happening.

Declan is not addressed directly. He is too young for explanation. This is stated out loud. He will not understand. This justification allows the visit to proceed without speaking to him.

One of the social workers asks Jemma to put Declan down so they can help him get ready. Jemma hesitates. Her arms tighten around him.

Declan reacts immediately. He stiffens. His legs draw up. His hand grips harder.

His body knows something is wrong before anyone touches him.

Jemma lowers him slowly. She pauses before his feet reach the floor. His grip tightens. She holds him there for a moment longer. When his feet touch the floor, his body stays tense. He stays close to her legs. He does not explore the room. He looks at the door.

The social worker crouches to his level. She says his name softly. She does not reach out yet. She waits. This waiting is intentional. It is meant to be gentle.

Declan does not respond. He does not look at her. His eyes stay fixed on Jemma.

They ask Jemma to gather some things. Clothes. A comfort item, if there is one. She moves stiffly. Her hands shake as she opens drawers. She does not know what to take. She takes too much, then puts things back.

Declan watches her move around the room. His breathing quickens. He begins to make a low sound. Not a cry. A sound held in the throat.

When Jemma moves out of sight, Declan's distress rises sharply. He folds in on himself. He crouches. His hands come up to his chest. The sound breaks into a cry then, sudden and high.

The social worker reaches for him then.

He recoils. His arms flail briefly, then lock tight against his sides. His back arches. He cries harder now, breath hitching between sounds. He is bracing.

The social worker lifts him carefully. There is a brief pause as his weight shifts between them. He resists the change in hold. She supports his weight properly. She speaks softly. He does not register safety.

He screams when he is lifted. It is not a long scream. It is sharp. It cuts off quickly as his breath catches. He shakes.

Jemma turns back into the room at the sound. She freezes. For a second, she looks like she might move forward. Then she stops. She puts her hands to her mouth. She does not speak.

He reacts as if this has happened before. His muscles are tight. His head pulls back. His eyes are wide. He does not cling. He does not settle against the person holding him. He is waiting for something else to happen.

The social worker adjusts her hold. She keeps her voice low. She says his name again. She says it will be OK. Jemma is asked if she wants to say goodbye. The question is gentle. It assumes a choice. The reality does not.

Jemma steps forward. She reaches out. Her hand hovers.

Then it makes contact.

Declan sees her move and cries again, louder this time. He twists towards her. His arms extend, then pause mid-air, then pull back.

She touches his face. Her hands shake. She tells him she loves him. She tells him she will see him soon. She tells him to be good. The words tumble out without structure.

He understands the tone.

He understands that she is upset. His crying intensifies. He jerks against the hold of the social worker.

The social worker holds firm but gently. She does not let go. Another worker opens the door. The air from outside comes in. He reacts again. He cries harder. His legs kick weakly. His energy is already draining.

Jemma follows them to the door. She keeps talking. She keeps touching him until she is told gently that it is time. She steps back. The door closes slowly with care. The latch clicks. Footsteps fade down the stairwell.

Inside the stairwell, his crying changes. It becomes rhythmic. Less sharp. He is still tense, but the initial shock has passed.

The workers move efficiently. They speak quietly to each other. They do not discuss the case. They focus on getting to the car safely. He is placed in a car seat. The straps are adjusted. Each click of the buckle makes him flinch. He cries again when he is restrained. He does not fight now. He sags slightly. The crying becomes softer, then stops.

He goes quiet.

The car pulls away.

The flat disappears from view. He stares at the ceiling of the car. His breathing is uneven. He remains tense. His hands clench and unclench slowly.

Inside the flat, Jemma sinks onto the floor. The room is still. The space where he stood is empty. No movement. No sound. The air holds.

The file will describe the visit as calm. Polite. No resistance. Child settled quickly. The decision had been made long before this morning. It was finalised in meetings with papers and signatures. He never attended those meetings. His consent was never considered. His body gave its answer anyway.

By the time the car reaches its destination, he is silent. His eyes are open. He does not sleep. He watches.

The visit is over. The procedure is complete. The next stage begins. He is taken from one place to another without explanation. His body will remember the moment.

The words used to justify it will fade from the file.

Unsupervised Knowing

When the door closes, the flat settles almost immediately. The sound of footsteps fades down the stairwell. The echo of voices disappears. The rooms return to their ordinary shape. There are no more chairs pulled in close. No notebooks resting on knees. No one choosing words with care.

Jemma stands where she was left. The space where Declan had been moments before feels larger than it should. His toys are still on the floor. His cup is on the table. Nothing has been cleared away. Nothing has been prepared for absence. The removal happened inside the life that was already in motion.

There is a moment where she does not move at all. Then she bends and sits on the floor. She presses her hands into her thighs as if to keep herself there. The flat is still. No crying. No movement. The silence is complete.

No one is watching now. No one is listening. The pressure to perform has vanished. The house exhales in a way that feels almost physical.

James returns later. He asks where Declan is. Jemma answers. The conversation is short.

There is anger.

There is blame.

There is relief.

There is no plan.

The file moves on immediately. The visit is written up. Calm. Cooperative. No resistance. A child distressed but settled. New headings are opened. Placement. Contact. Review dates. Timescales are set. Tasks are assigned. The language shifts to the future without pausing in the present.

There is no space in the file for the minutes after the door closed. No section for what happens in the room once the professionals leave. The case moves forward. Meetings are scheduled. Emails are sent. The focus shifts to what comes next.

For Declan, there is no after. There is only movement.

He is in a car. Then another building. Then another room. Each transition happens without explanation. Adults lift him, buckle him, carry him, place him down. Their voices are gentle. Their hands are careful. His body is still reacting to the last moment he understood. The moment when he was taken from the only environment he knows. He has no language for this. The sudden separation. The unfamiliar smells. The different temperature. The absence of the sounds that usually fill his days.

He stays tense. His muscles do not relax when he is placed down. He does not explore the room. He watches. He listens. He waits.

When someone reaches for him, his body tightens again. His breath changes. He does not cry loudly. He makes small sounds that stop quickly. The adults around him talk quietly. They explain what they are doing to each other. They do not explain it to him. Even if they did, his body would not understand.

He is given food. He takes it, but slowly. He stops often. He watches the face in front of him rather than the bottle. He does not settle into the rhythm of feeding. When he is changed, he stiffens. His legs resist being lifted. His hands grip at the air. The person changing him speaks softly and moves slowly. It does not undo what his body expects.

Sleep does not come easily. When he does sleep, it is shallow. His body jerks awake at small sounds. His breathing stays uneven. He does not sink into rest.

His body still responds as if harm is imminent. He flinches when someone moves too quickly. He freezes when a door opens. He watches hands carefully. The adults caring for him notice this. They describe him as guarded. As sensitive. As needing time.

The file records his placement. It notes that he arrived distressed. It notes that he settled after a short period. No one writes that he stopped crying because his body shut down. No one writes that quiet is not calm.

Jemma does not see this. She does not know what his nights are like. She does not see how he reacts to being held. She does not see the way he startles in sleep. She is not told.

Contact arrangements will be discussed later.

In the flat, Declan's absence becomes more pronounced as the hours pass. His sounds are missing. The rhythms that were built around him collapse. Meals happen without interruption. Sleep happens without waking.

The flat feels lighter. It brings guilt. It brings relief. It brings both at once.

The system does not sit with this contradiction. The focus now is on compliance with the next stage. On assessments. On timelines. On future decisions.

For Declan, the rupture is ongoing.

He does not know that the adults who hurt him are no longer there. He does not know that he is safe. In the hours after the visit, Declan learns nothing new except that separation happens without warning. That adults come and go. That crying does not bring return.

The file reflects this by moving on. The focus shifts forward. The language becomes technical again. Placement stability. Attachment. Long-term planning. These words appear in neat lines.

The pain of the moment is already receding from the record.

Declan lives entirely inside that pain for now. He does not mark time. He does not understand days. The present is disorientation. The present is vigilance.

When someone reaches for him gently and nothing bad happens, his body does not trust it yet. The system will measure progress by observable change. By sleep patterns. By feeding. By behaviour.

The file will not capture the cost of waiting. It will not capture the way fear settles into muscle and bone. It will not capture how long it takes for a body to believe what a file assumes.

On one side, professionals plan. They review. They schedule. They speak about Declan in meetings he will never attend.

On the other side, Declan exists in a present that has no after yet. Only a before that ended suddenly and a now that does not make sense.

The door closed.

The system moved on.

Arrival

The handover takes place in a council building that looks like every other one Declan has already passed through. Neutral walls. Worn chairs. A smell that sits somewhere between cleaning fluid and old coffee. It is warm but not comfortable. The kind of place designed to keep people moving rather than staying.

The social worker arrives with a folder tucked under one arm. The folder is thick. It contains dates, summaries, injuries, decisions. Declan arrives too, but not with her. He is carried by someone whose role is already ending. A transport worker. A temporary adult. Someone who has learned not to linger.

There is no formal goodbye. No explanation offered to Declan. No moment marked out as significant. He is passed from one set of arms to another with the efficiency of a process that has been practised many times before. The exchange takes seconds. The paperwork takes longer.

His name is said aloud once, quietly, to confirm identity. The carers repeat it back, softer. They say it as if volume might matter. As if saying it gently could make the moment less sharp.

Declan does not respond. He stays still in the arms holding him. His eyes are open. His face does not change.

He arrives with a nappy bag and a plastic carrier. The bag is light. Too light for a child his age. Inside are a few nappies. Not enough for a full day. A bottle. A jumper. Some clothes folded quickly, creased in places where hands pressed them down rather than smoothed them out.

The clothes are mismatched. Different sizes. Some already too small. One item smells faintly of bleach. Another smells of something sour. There is no spare set. No weather-appropriate layers. Nothing chosen with care.

There is a comfort toy, if it can be called that. A soft thing with flattened fur and no distinct smell. It does not carry the scent of a person or a place. It feels recently handled but not cherished.

There is a dummy with a small crack at the side. It is still in use. No one comments on it.

The bag has been packed in a rush, or with indifference. Either way, it contains what was nearby rather than what was needed.

The foster carers take the bag and then take Declan. They do not ask questions yet. They know there will be time for that later. They know this room is not the place. The social worker is still speaking, still reading from the folder.

She talks about the plan. About placement. About review dates. About contact to be discussed. Her tone is steady. Procedural. She does not rush, but there is no pause for emotion.

She mentions routines briefly. She says he has not had consistent ones. She suggests keeping things calm. She suggests predictability. These are recommendations, not instructions.

The carers nod. They have heard this before. They understand that this is the beginning, not the explanation.

They do not ask about the bruises. About the cupboard. About the fridge. About the chest injury. About James. About what was seen and when and by whom. They know the answers will be partial at best.

That information is in the file. And what is missing is, for now, not theirs to know.

Declan sits on a knee while the adults talk. He does not lean into the body holding him. He does not pull away. He sits upright, supported but not resting. His posture is too controlled for a child his age.

He does not cry. He does not fuss. He does not reach for the bag or the toy. He looks around the room slowly, deliberately. His gaze pauses at corners. At doorways. At faces.

His body is too still. His face does not shift much. There is no overt distress. There is no visible relief either.

He is dirty. There is grime under his fingernails. His clothes are stiff. His skin feels dry when touched. These details are noticed immediately by the carers. They do not comment out loud.

The social worker finishes what she needs to say. She asks if there are any questions.

There are none yet. The carers know better than to ask them now. She leaves. The folder goes with her.

The door closes. The sound of it echoes briefly down the close and then disappears.

The room feels different immediately. Quieter. Less purposeful. The carers shift their weight. One of them stands. The other adjusts their hold on Declan.

The building no longer feels like a place of transition. It feels like a place where nothing else will happen.

They gather their things and leave.

The drive is short. Declan sits in the car seat without resistance. His body does not relax into it. He tolerates the straps. He does not cry when they are fastened. He does not protest. He watches the movement of hands closely until the door is shut.

The car moves. Declan does not look out of the window. He stares at the seat in front of him.

When they arrive at the house, the carers move slowly. They speak quietly. They say his name again as they lift him. Softly.

Inside, the house feels lived in. Not pristine. Not chaotic. Ordinary. Declan is carried through rooms and set down on the living room floor. He does not crawl away. He stays where he is placed.

The carers sit nearby. They do not crowd him. They do not fill the silence with noise. They let the room settle.

Declan scans faces again. His eyes move quickly, then stop. He watches hands. He listens for sounds beyond the room.

He does not cry. He does not explore. He does not test. He remains still.

The carers exchange a look. Not panic. Recognition.

They do not try to make him laugh. They do not clap or sing. They do not push toys into his hands. They place a few objects on the floor within reach and wait.

He does not reach for them.

They lift him again after a while and carry him to the kitchen. Food is prepared. Something simple. Warm. He is offered it slowly.

He eats, but not eagerly. He takes a few mouthfuls and then stops. He watches the adult rather than the food. He waits.

The carers leave the food there. They do not remove it. After a minute, he eats again. Slowly. Carefully. He stops often.

When he is finished, he does not signal. He simply stops moving his mouth.

Afterwards, they change his nappy. His body stiffens slightly when lifted. He tolerates the handling. He does not relax into it. When he is put down again, there is a small release of tension.

Later, when the house is quiet, they go through the bag properly.

They find the bottle with sour milk inside. They empty it and rinse it without comment.

They find clothes that are too small. They set them aside.

They find the jumper that smells faintly of bleach. They smell it again, as if checking their own reaction.

They do not find information about bedtime, or feeding preferences, or comfort objects. There is no note about what helps him settle. There is no note about what frightens him.

There is a piece of paper with his date of birth. There is a list of injuries.

The injuries are listed clinically. Bruising. Weight loss. Under stimulation. Suspected non-accidental injury. Multiple attendances. The language is flat. It is familiar to the carers. They have seen this before.

What unsettles them is not the injuries themselves. It is how ordinary they appear on the page. How contained. How manageable they seem in words.

Those words do not describe the feel of his skin. Dry. Slightly cool. They do not describe the way his limbs hesitate before movement, as if checking for permission.

They do not describe the way he flinches when someone reaches too quickly, even gently. The way his eyes widen for a fraction of a second before his face stills again.

They do not describe the effort it takes for him to remain present.

The carers carry him back to the living room. They sit with him. They stay quiet. They let time pass.

They begin to understand what the file cannot say.

This is not a child reacting to a single event. This is not a child unsettled by change alone. This is a child whose body has been shaped by repetition. By harm that was frequent enough to become expected.

This is not new harm. This is old harm left unattended.

New Placement, Old Fears

They feed him first because it feels like the right place to start. Hunger is the simplest thing to address, the most concrete. The bottle is prepared carefully. The water is checked twice. The milk is measured properly. They do not rush, even though there is a quiet urgency in the room.

When the bottle is offered, Declan takes it immediately. There is no hesitation. His mouth latches hard and fast. He drinks with an intensity that surprises them. There is no pause, no moment where he pulls back to breathe or rest. His hands grip the bottle clumsily, fingers tight, knuckles pale. He drinks as if the milk might be taken away at any second.

One of the carers tilts the bottle slightly to slow the flow. She speaks softly, telling him to take his time, even though she knows he cannot understand the words. His sucking does not change. He keeps going until they gently pull the bottle away to let him breathe. He gasps once, quickly, then settles back into drinking the moment it is returned.

They watch him closely. They are experienced enough to know this is not how most children feed when they feel secure. They exchange a look, brief and quiet. Neither of them says what they are thinking. They are not sure yet if this urgency comes from hunger or memory. They suspect it is both.

When the bottle is empty, Declan gives no sign that he is finished. He keeps sucking until there is nothing left. When the bottle is removed, his mouth continues the motion for a second too long before he realises. He looks up then, eyes wide, checking faces. When nothing bad happens, his shoulders drop slightly.

They hold him upright for a while. He does not relax against them. His body stays engaged, as if he expects to be put down abruptly. He burps quietly. He does not fuss. He makes no sound at all.

After feeding, they decide to clean him properly. It feels important. Necessary. His clothes come off easily. They are worn thin. Some are damp with old spills. When the fabric is lifted away, his skin is revealed fully for the first time.

There are marks. Some are fading. Yellowing bruises that have begun to heal. Others are newer. Blue and purple, still defined. There are small scratches. Areas of redness. Places where the skin looks sore and irritated. There are patterns that do not look accidental.

They say nothing aloud.

They do not need to. They are both looking at the same things.

They carry him to the bathroom and begin to run the bath. The water fills slowly. They test it once, then again, even though they already know the temperature is right. Tonight, everything feels like it matters more.

Declan does not resist the bath. He does not cry when he is lowered into the water. He does not splash. He does not reach for toys. He sits where he is placed, legs bent slightly, hands resting on his thighs. His back is straight. His eyes are open.

The carers wait for some sign of engagement. A kick. A splash. A sound.

Nothing comes.

They wash him gently. They speak quietly, naming what they are doing. They pour water slowly over his shoulders. He does not flinch, but he does not respond either. His body remains alert. When water runs over his chest, his breathing changes slightly. It becomes quicker. One of the carers notices and slows down further.

The bath ends without incident. When they lift him out, his body goes rigid immediately. His arms pull inward. His legs stiffen. It takes time for him to settle into the towel. Even then, his muscles stay tense beneath the fabric. He does not mould himself into the hold. He allows it without trusting it.

They dry him carefully. They avoid any rough movements. They dress him slowly. His limbs do not offer themselves to sleeves or trouser legs. He does not push his arm through when guided. He does not resist. He simply waits for it to be done.

When they pick him up again, his arms stay close to his body. His hands remain in fists. He looks past the faces around him, fixing his gaze on the ceiling light. He does not seek eye contact. He does not avoid it either. Faces seem to be something to monitor rather than engage with.

They carry him to the bedroom. The cot is ready. Clean sheets. A soft toy placed carefully to one side. A small night light casting a low glow. The basics are all there. Everything that is supposed to help.

They lay him down gently.

He does not cry. He does not protest. He lies there, eyes open, staring up. His body remains still.

Too still.

His breathing is shallow but steady. He does not move his head to follow them as they step back.

They wait.

They stand just outside the doorway at first, listening. Expecting a sound. A whimper. A cry. Something that signals distress.

Nothing comes.

They check the monitor. He is still awake, eyes open. Unmoving. Minutes pass. Then more.

One of them goes back into the room and stands beside the cot. Declan blinks slowly. His eyes track the movement, but his body does not shift. He does not reach up. He does not turn away.

He looks like a child who is measuring something. Not the room, but the situation. As if he is trying to work out whether this place is real. Whether it will last. Whether sleep is safe here.

The carer does not speak. She does not touch him. She simply stands there for a moment, letting him see her. Then she steps back out again.

They leave the door slightly open.

The house settles into night. The usual sounds arrive. The hum of appliances. The distant noise of traffic. None of it is loud. None of it is threatening.

Declan remains awake.

Eventually, his eyes close, but his body does not relax. His fists stay clenched. His shoulders remain raised. His sleep, when it comes, is shallow. He startles once, sharply, then goes still again.

He does not cry out.

Later, much later, when the house is quiet and the night feels settled, the carers sit at the kitchen table. They do not turn on the main light. They speak softly, even though Declan cannot hear them from where they are.

They begin to list what they have seen.

The way he drank the bottle. The urgency. The way he did not stop on his own. The way his body stayed tense even when held gently. The marks on his skin. The way he sat in the bath without moving. The way he lay in the cot without making a sound.

They do not use professional language. They do not label anything yet. They speak as people trying to understand what has just arrived in their care.

They struggle to find words that feel accurate. Every word seems either too soft or too clinical. Too small for what they are holding.

Eventually, they stop trying to name it. They sit with the discomfort instead.

They know it, even if they cannot articulate it properly yet.

This is a child who does not expect to be comforted. This is a child who has learned that crying does not bring relief. That making noise does not change outcomes. That staying quiet costs less.

They do not say this out loud. They do not need to.

One of them gets up and checks the monitor again. Declan is still asleep. Or something close to it. His body has not shifted.

They turn the monitor volume up slightly, just in case.

When they return to bed, sleep does not come easily for them either. They lie awake, listening. Waiting for a sound that does not come.

The first night passes without drama. No crying. No calling out. No disruption.

On paper, it would look like a success.

In the house, it feels anything but.

They know that what they have witnessed is not calm. It is not adjustment. It is not resilience.

It is a child who has learned to endure.

And endurance, they know, is not the same thing as safety.

Bruising on back. "Apparently knocked down by a car today. Mother advises the driver grazed Declan."

Social Worker Home Visit Record, 1983

Learning His Body

Over the next few days, the carers begin to notice things the paperwork does not show. The file lists injuries and dates. It does not show how quickly Declan's breathing changes. It does not show how little warning his body gives.

His signals are small. His breathing shifts first. It becomes faster, higher. His shoulders rise. His hands curl inward, fingers tightening against his palms. If these signs pass unnoticed, he does not cry anymore. He becomes still. His movements slow. His weight settles heavily into whoever is holding him. If they wait longer than that, his body stiffens, and holding him becomes harder, not easier.

When someone enters the room while he is playing, he stops. He looks up immediately. His eyes fix on the adult's face. He waits. Sometimes he does not return to what he was doing, even after the person sits down.

Sleep shows this most clearly.

One night, they find him awake in the cot, sitting upright in the dark. He is silent. His hands rest flat on the mattress. His back is straight. He does not move when they enter. He watches them without reaching out.

When the carer lifts him, his body stiffens at once. His breathing is shallow. It takes time to slow. He does not settle against the chest holding him. When he is put back down, he lies with his eyes open long after the room is quiet again.

They begin to adjust how they move around him. They speak less while handling him. They slow their hands. They wait before lifting him. They give him time to register what is happening. They say what they are about to do, briefly and in the same order each time. I am picking you up. I am putting you down. I am leaving the room.

They notice how much space he needs.

During the day, the same pattern appears. He eats what is offered. He does not refuse. He allows himself to be held. He sits where he is placed. He does not resist. They do not treat this as ease. They pause before touching him. They give him room. They avoid crowding. When they move away, they do so slowly.

Sometimes he plays without looking up for a few seconds at a time. When this happens, they leave it undisturbed.

At night, the waking continues. Some nights he settles more quickly. Other nights he does not. When he is lifted, the stiffness still comes first. Sometimes it eases sooner. Sometimes it does not. They do not remark on these changes. They notice them and adjust.

They repeat the same sequences even when nothing seems to require it. Same order. Same pace. Same tone.

They do not expect progress to move in one direction.

They do not name what they are seeing. They do not call it healing. They learn what helps him stay present. How quickly he becomes overwhelmed. How long it takes before his body loosens after it has braced.

What they are learning is how much time his body needs before it believes what happens next.

Parallel Risks

The house is different as Declan is carried inside and set down, and the difference is felt rather than pointed out. Meals happen at the same time each day. Breakfast arrives without negotiation. Lunch follows whether he asks for it or not. Dinner comes while there is still light outside. Food is placed in front of him and left there long enough for him to decide what to do with it. No one hovers. No one rushes him. No one removes it the moment he looks away.

The lights stay on. Evenings do not slip into shadow without warning. Lamps are switched on before rooms go dark. Curtains are closed gently. There are no sudden plunges into darkness that demand vigilance.

Doors close quietly. They do not slam. They do not signal anger. When someone leaves a room, the door follows them with a soft click rather than a bang. This happens every time. It is not commented on.

Voices stay level, even when something spills, even when a cup tips over, even when Declan drops food on the floor. There is no sharp intake of breath. No raised voice. The mess is dealt with, and the moment passes.

Nothing is demanded immediately. No one insists that he smile. No one asks him to look up. No one pulls his chin gently to meet their eyes. When he looks away, that is accepted. When he stays still, that is accepted too. Closeness is offered, not imposed. Arms are open, not reaching. If he leans in, he is held. If he does not, the space remains. No one says come here. No one says it is fine. They wait.

Safety is present, but it is quiet. It does not announce itself. It does not prove itself with promises. It sits in repetition.

Declan does not respond to this as relief. He does not relax into it. He does not settle in the way the file expects settling to look.

He responds as if it might vanish.

He watches hands. He tracks movement. When someone stands up, his eyes follow them until they sit again. When footsteps sound in the hallway, his body stills. He listens. When food arrives, he eats quickly at first, then stops. He looks up between mouthfuls. He watches the adult at the table rather than the plate. He checks for reaction. He checks for change.

If the food remains untouched by adult hands, he eats a little more. Slowly. Carefully. He does not trust that it will stay.

When he is picked up, his body stiffens before it softens. The stiffness comes first every time. The softening takes longer. Sometimes it does not come at all.

The person holding him notices this. They adjust their hold. They speak quietly. They do not insist that he relax. They accept the tension as part of him rather than something to be corrected.

Sleep is harder. He lies down without protest, but his body does not sink. His eyes close, then open again. He wakes at small sounds: a floorboard, a car outside, a door in another room.

When he wakes, he does not cry immediately. He waits. He listens. He checks whether crying will bring someone or something else. This waiting is brief, but it is deliberate.

When someone comes, they come calmly. They do not flick on lights abruptly. They do not speak sharply. They lift him slowly. They hold him without bouncing or jostling.

Sometimes he cries then. Sometimes he does not. Sometimes his body shakes even when his voice stays quiet.

The house responds the same way each time. There is no frustration. No escalation. No withdrawal.

Days pass like this. Repetition without drama. Meals. Sleep. Play. Quiet voices. Gentle hands.

Declan does not rush to trust this. He does not test it loudly. He tests it in small ways. He drops food deliberately and watches what happens. He knocks over a toy and waits. He makes a noise and then stops to see the response.

The responses are consistent. Nothing bad happens.

Still, he remains alert.

Trust is not part of the placement agreement. It is not listed in the paperwork. It does not appear under outcomes or objectives. It cannot be scheduled or reviewed.

The adults caring for him understand this without saying it. They do not expect affection. They do not interpret distance as rejection. They know that time is required, but they do not rush it.

They speak to him as if he understands more than he can say. They explain what they are doing even when he does not look at them. They narrate small actions. I am going to lift you now. I am going to change you. I am here.

These words are repeated. They land slowly.

Declan begins to anticipate some of the routines. He knows when food is coming. He knows when the lights will dim. He knows which footsteps belong to which person. This knowledge reduces the need for constant scanning.

He still watches hands.

When a door closes gently, he startles less than before. The reaction is still there, but it fades faster. His body takes note.

The house holds its shape. It does not change depending on mood. This consistency matters more than comfort.

No one praises him for coping. No one comments on how well he is doing. There is no expectation that he should be grateful. He is allowed to be as he is.

When he cries, it is responded to. When he is quiet, it is simply noticed.

The file will later describe this as settling. It will note improved routine, reduced distress, positive placement.

What it will not capture is the effort it takes for Declan to remain present in his body. The vigilance that has not yet left him. The way his muscles stay ready even during calm.

The other house does not demand change from him. It offers repetition instead.

Over time, he begins to test proximity. He crawls a little closer during play. He leans against a leg without fully committing his weight. He looks up briefly, then away.

Each time, nothing bad happens.

This is how trust begins, if it begins at all. Not with declarations. Not with relief. With the absence of harm repeated often enough to be noticed.

There are moments when the past intrudes sharply. A raised voice from outside the house. A loud noise from the street. Declan's body reacts immediately. His breathing changes. His shoulders rise.

The adults notice. They lower their voices further. They name what happened. That was a loud noise. You are safe. They do not insist that he believe them. They sit with him until his body settles again.

He does not ask questions. He does not have language for them. He carries them physically.

The house does not try to erase where he came from. It does not need to. It simply does not repeat it. There is no shouting. No sudden movements. No unpredictable absence. The doors that close also open again.

The file will eventually speak about attachment, about progress, about outcomes. These words will appear as summaries.

Declan experiences none of this as progress. He experiences it as waiting. Waiting to see if the routine holds. Waiting to see if the tone stays the same. Waiting to see if kindness comes with conditions.

The days accumulate quietly. One meal after another. One night after another. Nothing dramatic happens.

This is the point.

Safety is offered without proof, without demand, without deadline. Declan does not yet accept it. He observes it. He allows it to exist around him while keeping his body ready. Trust cannot be instructed. It cannot be rushed. It cannot be recorded in the way other changes can.

The other house knows this.

It does not ask for trust.

It waits.

It keeps quiet, making space for the possibility of trust without demanding it. The house attends to presence, not promises. No grand gestures. Only the slow repetition of safety, of routine, of gentle voices. It lets Declan observe, lets him notice. It offers patience, holding its breath while he decides what to accept and what to hold back. The house understands what cannot be forced.

It settles into waiting, offering steadiness in place of certainty. The days pass, the rooms remain unchanged, and the doors continue to open as they always have. Trust, if it arrives, will come quietly, almost imperceptibly, as the absence of harm continues.

Who Holds, Who Lets Go

When he is lifted, his body stiffens before anything else happens. The change is immediate. His muscles tighten as soon as hands come under his arms. His shoulders rise. His spine curves slightly backwards. His arms do not relax around the person holding him. They stay close to his sides or press awkwardly against the adult's chest.

The adults caring for him notice this early. They mention it to each other. Even then, his body responds the same way. The stiffness comes first. Any softening, if it comes at all, arrives later and only partially. When he is carried from one room to another, his eyes stay wide. He keeps his head upright. His breathing becomes quicker, more shallow.

Sudden movement startles him. Someone standing up too quickly. A door opening without warning. His shoulders jerk. His back tightens. He does not cry loudly. He becomes still. He watches. His eyes move from face to face, from doorway to doorway, until the room settles again.

Touch does not soothe him. He does not melt into arms. He does not lean his weight fully against the person holding him. He tolerates being held. He allows it. His body remains alert.

When someone strokes his back or rubs his arm, he does not pull away, but he does not respond either. He can be held for a long time without changing posture. His muscles stay engaged.

When he is put down, there is a brief release. His shoulders drop slightly. His breathing slows. The change is small but visible to those watching closely. Being on the floor feels safer than being in arms.

He startles in his sleep. His body jerks suddenly. His eyes open immediately. When he wakes, he lies still and listens before making any sound.

If someone comes quickly, he may cry briefly. If they take longer, he often stays silent. These patterns are observed over days and weeks. They remain consistent.

In notes and meetings, his reactions are described carefully. Tense. Difficult to soothe. Sensitive to noise. The word behaviour appears. Interventions are suggested. Gentle handling. Predictable routines. Quiet environments. These are already in place.

No one documents what it feels like to lift a child whose body prepares for harm every time it leaves the ground.

The carers adjust how they hold him. They put him down when his body tightens too much. They move slowly. They do not force closeness. They notice small changes and do not comment on them.

He continues to be held gently. He continues to stiffen. He continues to watch.

The gap remains.

Learning Safety

Care is consistent. Food arrives before hunger escalates. Meals are not delayed as a test. They are not earned. They simply appear, at roughly the same times each day, in the same place, served in the same way. There is no announcement, no emphasis. Predictability itself is the point.

When adults leave the room, they say so. When they come back, they do it when they said they would.

He still checks.

Calm feels provisional to him. He behaves as if it might be withdrawn. He does not associate safety with warmth or affection. He associates it with predictability. With nothing bad happening when nothing bad was expected. With adults doing what they said they would do.

Learning safety is slow. It does not move forward in obvious stages. Some days he seems more relaxed. Other days he returns to scanning, to stiffness, to withdrawal. The carers do not rush these days. They do not treat them as failures.

They do not take his withdrawal personally. When he pulls away from touch, they do not insist. When he does not respond to affection, they do not withdraw theirs. They remain present. They do not expect eye contact. They do not insist on closeness. They do not measure progress by affection returned.

They measure different things.

How long he plays before stopping. How often he checks faces. How quickly his body settles after a startle.

They narrate their actions even when it seems unnecessary. I am going to the other room. I will be back. I am picking you up now. I am putting you down.

Declan does not respond to the words. His body responds to their accuracy.

What he learns is that fewer bad things are happening. That certain patterns repeat. That absence does not automatically lead to harm. This settles slowly. When his reactions return, the stiffening, the scanning, the withdrawal. They pass more quickly now than they once did.

This requires adults who do not expect gratitude. Who do not frame progress as compliance. Who do not withdraw care when it is not reciprocated.

Declan continues to give compliance. He follows routines. He allows care. He does what is expected of him. This could be mistaken for ease. The carers know it is not.

They offer choices where possible. Which book. Which cup. Which toy. At first, he does not respond. He waits. Over time, he begins to point. Tentatively. Then more clearly.

They remain consistent even when it feels like nothing is changing. Calm still does not hold. He still checks. He still startles. He recovers more quickly.

Safety is no longer only the absence of immediate threat. It begins to include the presence of predictable care.

It is happening in small, ordinary moments.

Residual Harm

What remains cannot be photographed. It does not sit neatly in case notes or appear in summary documents. It does not announce itself during reviews or surface cleanly in meetings. It waits instead in muscle and breath, in the small spaces between action and reaction, in the pauses that are too brief to attract concern but too consistent to be coincidence.

Declan sleeps, but sleep does not look like rest. His body lies still, but the stillness is held, not surrendered. His breathing remains shallow even in deeper stages of sleep. His limbs do not sprawl. His hands stay close to his body. There is no softness to the posture. It is readiness, practised and precise.

When something shifts in the room, even quietly, his body responds. A change in air. A footstep in the hallway. A door closing two rooms away. His muscles tighten before his eyes open. Sometimes they do not open at all. The response happens anyway.

In waking moments, he carries the same readiness. It is subtle. Easy to miss. He does not flinch dramatically when touched. There is no recoil that demands explanation. Instead, there is a fraction of a second where his body stiffens, where breath catches, where his shoulders rise just enough to show that contact is being assessed before it is accepted.

Hands arrive with conditions. His body learned this long before language. Touch once meant something unpredictable. Sometimes care. Sometimes pain. Sometimes restraint. Sometimes nothing at all. That uncertainty lives on in the way he receives closeness now.

When someone reaches for him, he watches the hand first. He tracks the movement. He notices speed, angle, intention. Only after this assessment does he allow the contact to continue. This process happens quickly, almost invisibly, but it happens every time.

Closeness is monitored rather than sought. He allows people near him, but he does not lean into them. He sits beside rather than against. If an arm settles around him, his body stays upright. He does not shift his weight fully. He remains balanced, prepared to move if needed.

He watches mood in silence. He tracks faces closely. A slight change in tone. A tightening around the mouth. A raised eyebrow. These signals matter to him. They always have. He responds to them without drawing attention to himself.

He does not ask for reassurance. He does not complain. He does not test boundaries loudly. He complies. Compliance feels safer than curiosity. It costs less.

At reviews, he is described as quiet. As settled. As managing. These words are accurate if they are taken at face value. They do not describe the work happening underneath.

His quietness is active. Maintained rather than natural. It requires constant monitoring of his environment.

There is no checkbox for learned fear. No tick box for vigilance. No section that asks how much effort it takes for a child to remain still, agreeable, manageable.

There are questions about behaviour. About sleep. About attachment. These questions circle the edges of what remains without naming it.

When professionals observe him, they see a child who does not demand much. He does not cry excessively. He does not act out. He does not draw attention to himself. This is read as progress.

What is missed is the cost of this progress. The energy it takes to stay contained. The way his body remains on alert even in calm spaces. The way safety is experienced as temporary rather than assured.

In moments of stress, what remains becomes more visible. A loud voice. A sudden movement. A raised hand that is meant as a gesture but reads as threat. His body reacts instantly. The calm disappears. The vigilance sharpens.

These moments pass more quickly now than they once did. That is also progress. The reaction itself remains. It simply recedes faster.

The carers understand this. They respond consistently. They do not take it personally when he withdraws. They do not interpret distance as rejection. They do not rush to fill silence.

They have learned that presence matters more than reassurance. That predictability matters more than affection. That staying matters more than explaining.

Still, what remains does not belong only to the present. It will travel with him into future spaces. Into classrooms. Into friendships. Into moments of intimacy and conflict he cannot yet imagine.

It will shape how he responds to authority. How he experiences closeness. How he handles disagreement. How he reads people.

He may become adept at managing adults. At anticipating needs. At staying agreeable. These skills will be praised. They may even be rewarded.

What will stay hidden is the vigilance underneath. The way his body never fully rests. The way calm always feels provisional.

No one will write that down. It does not fit the form.

Files will note improvement. Stability. Reduced concern. These words will appear in closing summaries. They will signal resolution.

What remains will not be resolved.

It will surface in moments that seem disproportionate. In reactions that do not make sense without context. In a body that reacts faster than thought.

This is not pathology. It is memory. Not the kind that can be recalled and described, but the kind that lives in muscle, breath, and posture.

It is what happens when fear is learned early and often enough to become automatic.

What remains is quiet. It does not announce itself. It does not demand attention. It sits just beneath the skin, shaping responses.

The body learns quickly when it is not safe to be heard.

I know this because I carried it once too.

I know how stillness can look like calm from the outside while everything inside stays alert. I know how hands can register as risk before they register as comfort. I know how silence can feel safer than sound.

I know how compliance can be mistaken for trust.

What remains does not make someone broken. It makes them careful. It makes them skilled in ways that are rarely recognised as survival.

Declan will grow around this. He will adapt. He will learn new patterns. Some of the vigilance will soften. Some of it will stay.

The goal is not to erase what remains. That is neither possible nor necessary. The goal is to give him enough safety, enough consistency, enough time, that what remains no longer has to work so hard.

That it can rest sometimes. That it can find moments of ease, where the weight lessens and the urgency fades. It can loosen its grip, allowing space for gentleness and the possibility of peace. That the constant vigilance may pause, even if only briefly, and make room for something softer.

It can become part of his history rather than the thing that governs his present.

What remains is quiet. It is persistent. It is real. And it deserves to be named, even if it cannot be recorded.

Monsters in the System

They do not always look monstrous. They are rarely loud or visibly cruel. They do not announce themselves with obvious threat. Often they look tired. They look like people who know how to sit still in a chair and wait their turn.

They arrive on time, or close enough. They answer questions and explain themselves. They use words that sound right. They understand the shape of the conversation and adjust to it. In rooms where professionals gather, they are often cooperative. They nod, agree, and express concern in appropriate ways. They talk about stress. About pressure. About feeling overwhelmed. These explanations are familiar. They move easily through the room.

They know when to apologise and when to deflect. How to sound regretful without saying very much. How to say the right thing without committing to change.

They offer explanations that are plausible enough to hold. They keep their stories consistent. Consistency matters more than accuracy.

In Declan's case, James learned this. He did not need to charm everyone. He only needed to avoid alarming them. He learned when to be present and when to disappear. He learned when silence was safer than speech.

He learned how to make himself look peripheral even when he was central. In meetings, his presence was described indirectly. Tension. Arguments. Relationship difficulties. His behaviour was discussed without being named. The language stayed general. His actions stayed abstract.

When violence is framed as difficulty, urgency fades. When control is described as concern, it becomes manageable. When fear is called stress, it fits existing categories. Effort becomes the focus. Attendance. Apologies. Partial compliance. Explanations that resemble familiar patterns.

Caution shapes this. Proportionality. The desire to avoid overreaction. These are built into how the system works. They create room for delay.

Empathy is present. It allows work to continue. Attention shifts when adults speak about their own histories and struggles. The focus widens. What happens elsewhere remains unseen. The most damaging moments do not occur in meetings or visits. They happen between them, after professionals leave.

The system works with what can be observed. Some people learn how to control that.

Assumptions about normality soften interpretation. Tired parents lose their temper. Stressed adults make mistakes. Relationships are difficult. These ideas are familiar. Often there is someone else in the home who draws focus. Someone more visible. Someone more obviously vulnerable. Attention shifts.

In the file, James appears and disappears. His name is noted, then fades. His presence is recorded, then sidelined. This inconsistency makes him harder to fix in place. Responsibility spreads. Multiple professionals. Multiple roles. Each working within limits. Action requires alignment. Delay becomes possible.

This does not require calculation in a dramatic sense. It requires attention. It requires learning what follows which action and adjusting. Sometimes it is deliberate. Sometimes it is reactive.

They are often part of ordinary life. They work. They socialise. They have friends. They do not stand out. When harm comes from someone who looks ordinary, it is harder to hold the idea.

Explanations fill the gap. Stress. Alcohol. Relationship breakdown. These are easier to work with than the possibility that someone can appear reasonable and still be violent.

They do not need to threaten or intimidate openly. They only need to avoid triggering alarm. Controlled irritation passes. Compliance smooths edges. In meetings, concern may be expressed. A desire for the child's well-being. Discomfort at implication. These moments slow things down.

Later, the word *manipulative* sometimes appears. It explains little. It shifts attention away from the conditions that allow harm to continue. When harm is finally named, it can feel sudden. From the outside, it looks abrupt. From inside the case, it has been moving slowly for some time.

After action is taken, attention moves on. The narrative closes. New work begins elsewhere.

What remains does not.

It is tempting to believe that harm comes from people who are obvious. That it announces itself. That it is easy to recognise and stop.

Often it is quieter than that.

Presentation is not proof. Cooperation is not safety. Reasonableness does not guarantee protection. Declan's experience sits in that gap. The system responded to what it could see. What mattered most stayed out of view.

The danger lies in assuming that what looks reasonable is safe.

That assumption costs time. And time, for a child living with violence, is not neutral.

What Was Seen, Missed and Normal

The system did see a great deal. Bruises were noticed when Declan was brought into clinics and hospitals. Weight loss was recorded carefully, plotted against expected gain, and discussed in relation to feeding routines and possible explanations. Changes in his behaviour were remarked upon, sometimes tentatively, sometimes with concern, and rarely dismissed outright. Observations were made, written down, and shared between professionals. The record shows attention, not absence.

Clinicians noted bruising on Declan's body in places that raised questions. The back. The chest. Behind the ears. These were seen. Measurements were taken. Colours were described. The age of the bruises was estimated. Photographs were sometimes taken. The language was careful and precise. The observations themselves were accurate.

Weight loss was also recognised. It appeared in growth charts and clinic letters. Declan's weight dipped and failed to recover in expected ways. This was discussed in relation to feeding, to routines, and to stress in the household. Advice was given. Follow-ups were arranged.

Behavioural changes were discussed repeatedly. His quietness. His withdrawal. His lack of expected distress. These were noted in different ways by different professionals. Some described him as settled. Others described him as unusually subdued. Still others remarked on his lack of engagement. These observations were present at the time.

Each observation was treated as a discrete event. A bruise was assessed in isolation. Weight loss was discussed in relation to feeding difficulties rather than harm. Behavioural change was framed as stress or temperament. Familiar explanations kept the concerns inside ordinary risk. The accuracy of what was seen did not translate into clarity when the observations were placed alongside one another.

Bruises were seen and discussed in meetings. Weight loss was recorded and contextualised. Behavioural changes were noted and described. Alongside these observations sat other phrases: engaging with services, complex family circumstances, no immediate risk identified. These phrases appear in the same documents.

What was seen was filtered through professional roles. Doctors assessed injuries within medical parameters. Police assessed incidents within criminal thresholds. Social workers assessed risk within child protection frameworks. Each role produced clarity within its own limits.

The record reflects this. It shows detail within categories and uncertainty between them. Information was present but distributed. Each professional held part of it. The bruises were there. The weight loss. The silence. These details appear across pages and dates. They were written down.

What did not occur was their assembly.

Familiar explanations absorbed what was seen, allowing each concern to remain manageable on its own. Over time, this manageability shaped response.

The system continued to observe.

What was missed was the child's timeline. The system works in weeks and months. The record compresses time. Entries appear ordered and paced. No document holds the duration between harm and response as lived.

The system did not record how long fear persisted between visits. It did not mark the stretch of time in which nothing changed. When read later, escalation appears gradual and measured.

What was missed was the point at which accumulation had already occurred. Responsibility remained distributed. Decisions were made within roles. No single document names the moment when waiting itself became part of the harm.

Declan's injuries did not require reinterpretation to exist. They required synthesis to be understood together. The file contains what was needed. It holds back from stating what the material already shows until later.

When the threshold was crossed, it was not because new information appeared. Existing information was read together.

That shift is difficult to locate in the record. It does not announce itself. It sits inside reports that remain accurate and professional.

What was seen is there. It is captured in the lines and boxes, in the words that mark attendance, injury, or concern. The record preserves what was observed, each detail entered with care, as if the act of noting might be enough. But documentation alone is limited; the very act of recording also fixes the boundaries of what is acknowledged.

What was missed sits between entries. It lives in the quiet gaps, in the silences that stretch from one report to the next. These blank spaces are not accidental; they accumulate as days pass, shaping the story in ways that are not immediately visible. The spaces between become as much a part of the narrative as what is written.

What became normal allowed both to coexist. The routine of documentation, the established patterns, meant that what was recorded and what was overlooked could sit side by side. Over time, the ordinary absorbed the extraordinary, and the file held both the clarity of what was seen and the uncertainty of what was missed. This equilibrium, precarious yet persistent, carried forward, shaping every page that followed.

Files

New pages are added at pace. Dates are entered with confidence. Decisions are recorded as facts rather than possibilities. The uncertainty that marked earlier entries is gone. The tone shifts. What was once tentative becomes declarative.

There is relief in this. It shows in the writing. Sentences shorten. Language firms up. The case has direction now. There is a placement. There are review dates. There are clear roles. The problem has been named in a way that allows it to be managed.

The file is organised carefully. Tabs separate sections. Chronology is updated. Key events are summarised at the front so that anyone opening it can understand the story quickly. This is considered good practice. It makes the case accessible. It allows new professionals to enter without having to read everything.

Complexity is reduced so it can be held.

In earlier pages, the writing moved in circles. Concerns were raised, softened, and revisited. Explanations overlapped. Contradictions sat side by side without resolution. Now the structure is cleaner. There is a before and an after. There is a clear turning point.

Pain becomes manageable because it is divided. An injury becomes an incident. An incident becomes a date. A date becomes an outcome. Each step creates distance. Each step makes the story easier to contain.

The injuries are still there on paper. Bruising is listed. Weight loss is recorded. Hospital attendances are noted. They no longer disrupt the narrative. They explain why action was taken. They no longer drive it.

Language changes once responsibility shifts. Words like risk and harm remain, but they are used differently. They sit in the past tense more often now. Risk was identified. Harm was addressed. Safeguarding measures are in place.

The file reflects this shift. There is confidence in the phrasing. Plans are written with certainty. Placement is described as stable. Contact is framed as structured. Progress is anticipated.

The system writes best when it feels resolved.

Meetings generate minutes that are clear and efficient. Decisions are summarised. Actions are allocated. There is less debate. There is more agreement. This is not because everyone suddenly understands everything. It is because the parameters have narrowed.

The file benefits from this narrowing. It can now do what it is designed to do. Track. Review. Evidence.

What cannot be contained on paper is quietly set aside.

There is no place to write about how Declan's body stiffens when lifted or how he scans faces before moving. These details appear occasionally in observation notes. They do not travel or shape decisions.

The file privileges what can be measured. Sleep duration. Feeding patterns. Attendance at contact. These are concrete. They can be compared over time. They can be graphed if needed.

Internal states resist this kind of tracking. They are mentioned briefly and then lost.

When professionals prepare reports, they select information that supports the current plan. This is not malicious. It is necessary. Reports have limits. They must be read in meetings with agendas. The file becomes selective without anyone deciding to be selective.

The file begins to tell a coherent story. It reads as if events unfolded logically, each leading to the next. The gaps and hesitations that marked the process are smoothed out. Decisions appear timely. Actions appear proportionate.

It suggests competence.

When staff change roles or move on, the file remains. It becomes the official memory. What is written carries more weight than what was felt.

New professionals entering the case read the summary first. They absorb the narrative as it is presented. They trust it. The language invites trust. It is measured. It is professional. It uses familiar frameworks. It cites legislation. It references guidance. It signals compliance with process.

The file can describe harm without conveying it. It can list injuries without evoking the body they happened to. It can describe fear without making the reader feel it. This is its function.

The file does not witness. It records.

As the file grows, some things become harder to find. Early notes are buried under later updates. Initial concerns are summarised rather than quoted. The language becomes more general.

What remains visible is what aligns with the current plan.

There are sections that remain thin. Emotional impact. Child experience. These headings exist, but they are often brief. They rely on interpretation rather than detail.

So these things are described obliquely or left aside.

The file becomes heavier, but not deeper. It contains more information, but less texture. The early messiness that reflected real uncertainty is replaced by clarity that reflects outcome rather than process.

This is how cases are closed eventually. With confidence. With summaries. With lessons-learned sections that speak in general terms.

The file will say that thresholds were eventually met. That action was taken. That Declan is now safe.

The file is not designed for accountability of feeling. It is designed for accountability of action. Once action has been taken, the file can relax. It can move towards closure.

The language reflects this. There is more forward planning. Less revisiting of the past. The case moves into a different category. Placement stability becomes the focus. Contact arrangements. Long-term outcomes. These are important. They deserve attention.

They also shift the gaze away from what happened.

The file grows heavier as it moves towards ending. Each review adds pages. Each decision adds documentation. The file does its job. It records what happened in a way that can be defended. It shows that action was taken when thresholds were met. It demonstrates compliance with procedure.

The file will one day be archived. It will sit on a server or in a storage room. It will be referenced if needed. It will not change.

"Four-point discoloration – Two areas of the ear. Consistent with N.A.I.
(Non-Accidental Injury) Blunt Force"

Health Visitor Note, NHS Records, 1984

Survival

There is no moment where it resolves. What comes after is quieter, less dramatic, and harder to describe. It is survival.

Declan grows. His body changes.

He learns routines. He learns how this house works, how these adults behave, what can be expected from a day. From the outside, this looks like progress. It is progress, in a limited sense. He is safer than he was. He is fed. He is warm. He is no longer being hurt. These things matter.

They do not erase what came before.

He learns how to live alongside what cannot be undone. His body learned fear early and learned it well. It still reacts to threat even when none is present. These adaptations are subtle. They look like personality. Like temperament. Like the way someone is.

Declan learns quickly what helps him get through the day. He learns which adults are predictable and which are not. He learns how to stay agreeable, how to avoid drawing attention when attention feels risky.

He learns when to speak and when to stay quiet. These skills serve him. They help him navigate spaces without incident. They are praised.

Teachers later describe him as well behaved. Calm. Mature for his age. He does what is asked. He does not demand much. These descriptions are offered with approval.

They are incomplete.

He functions. He adapts. He manages. This makes it easier for people to assume that time has done its work.

Time does some work. The sharpest edges soften. The reactions that once arrived instantly begin to slow. He startles less. He sleeps more deeply some nights. He learns that not every raised voice means danger. These changes are real.

What remains is quieter.

His body still responds before his mind does. In moments of stress, his shoulders tighten. His breathing changes. He scans the room without meaning to. He notices exits. He notices tone. He notices shifts in mood that others miss. This awareness becomes second nature.

As he grows older, this vigilance is sometimes mistaken for insight. He reads people well. He anticipates reactions. He avoids conflict. These are seen as strengths. They are also adaptations to an environment where misreading adults once carried consequences.

He does not talk much about his early life. It does not sit in his memory as a story. It exists in sensations, reactions, habits. There is nothing to recount cleanly.

When he is asked about his past in formal settings, the answers are short. I was in care. Things were hard. It was a long time ago. These statements are accepted. No one pushes.

The adults around him sometimes wonder why he struggles with closeness. Why he keeps a distance even with people he trusts. Why he seems uncomfortable when attention lingers. These questions are asked gently, if at all.

The answers, when they come, are framed in neutral terms. Attachment difficulties. Early trauma. These explanations are accurate enough. They allow understanding without requiring discomfort.

They do not capture how these patterns shape decision making, what feels safe and what does not. Declan learns to choose environments carefully. He prefers predictability. He avoids chaos. He is unsettled by volatility even when it is harmless. He feels responsible for keeping things steady. He takes it on automatically.

He carries these patterns forward into his adolescence, into his relationships, and into his work life, allowing them to shape how he interacts with those around him in each new phase.

He makes the effort to show up wherever he is needed, and he does not voice complaints, choosing instead to remain quietly resilient.

These characteristics are recognised and valued by others, as they reflect a dependable and steady presence.

However, maintaining these traits and behaviours often comes at a significant personal cost, which is not always visible to those around him.

Rest does not come easily. Even in safe spaces, his body remains partially alert. He finds it difficult to switch off completely. Silence can feel as tense as noise. Calm can feel temporary. These sensations are familiar. He lives with them.

People sometimes tell him how well he has done. How resilient he is. They mean it kindly. He does not know how to respond.

He did not bounce back. He adapted.

He learns which parts of himself to show and which to keep guarded. He understands that some things are carried rather than spoken. Being low maintenance helps keep relationships intact.

There are moments when the past breaks through more clearly. A sudden loss. A loud argument. A sense of being cornered. In these moments, his reactions feel disproportionate, even to him. His body reacts first. His thoughts follow.

No one taught him how to connect these reactions to what happened. The file did not travel with him in that way. He knows things were bad. He does not know how bad, or how long.

There is grief in this. Not always conscious, but present. It sits alongside daily life. It does not disrupt function. It informs it.

As he grows older, he becomes more aware of this pattern. He notices how quickly he adapts. How rarely he expects others to meet him emotionally. How often he meets them instead. This awareness brings mixed feelings. Pride. Sadness. Fatigue.

He builds a life that looks stable from the outside. It does not guarantee peace.

The scars he carries are not always visible. They show up in how he responds to stress, in how long it takes him to relax, and in how much effort goes into appearing fine.

The system that once surrounded him is largely gone from his daily life.

The file exists somewhere.

Archived.

The decisions that shaped his early years are no longer active. Their effects remain.

Declan lives with those traces.

This does not mean his life is defined by harm. It means harm is part of the context he carries forward. One influence among many. It does not dictate every outcome. It does shape some.

There are days when he feels almost ordinary. Days when the past feels distant. These days matter.

There are other days when the weight of what remains presses closer. When vigilance sharpens. When rest feels out of reach. These days pass too.

A door closes in another room.

His body notices before he does.

He stays still for a moment. The sound echoes faintly, weaving itself into the quiet. He senses the shift, his muscles taut, breath held, before understanding follows. It is a harmless noise, but his body treats it as a signal, a memory of vigilance that lingers. He waits for calm to return, lets the silence settle again, and only then allows himself to move.

Then he continues.

Acknowledgements

This book could not have been written without access to records held by public institutions. I am grateful to **National Records of Scotland** for guidance on my adoption records, and to staff at The **Mitchell Library** for assistance in locating archived material. I also acknowledge **West Dunbartonshire Health and Social Care Partnership** and **Argyll and Bute Health and Social Care**, whose records form part of the documentary basis of this work.

These acknowledgements do not imply endorsement of past decisions or systems, only recognition of access granted.

I owe particular thanks to **C. D.**, a social worker with Argyll and Bute Council, whose support over the past two years made this work possible. She prepared and reviewed extensive files, provided guidance through the adoption records process, and gave time and care to material that is difficult to hold. Her work was careful, thorough, and humane.

I acknowledge the **West Dunbartonshire Health and Social Care Partnership**, previously known as **Strathclyde Regional Council**, for its role in my placement, which positively altered the course of my life.

This book exists because of my adoptive parents, brother and sister.

My adoptive mum died before she could read my testament. Her absence was the point at which I began to look back, not out of dissatisfaction, but out of understanding. It was through losing her that I came to recognise the scale of what she and my adoptive father had done, the sacrifices they made, the care they gave, and the steadiness they provided without asking to be praised for it.

Her love was not loud. It did not depend on gratitude or return. It was practical, persistent and shaping. This book is not about her, but it is possible because of her. She was my safe space, my protector when the world around me was chaotic.

My adoptive father is acknowledged alongside her, for the same reasons. For staying. For choosing care repeatedly, quietly and without condition. My WWF Champion, my superhero. My DAD.

I thank my wife and my son, who anchor me in the present and remind me that care is not an abstract idea, but something lived daily, imperfectly and real.

Special thanks to Duncan, Chris, John, Gary, Natt and Grant for friendship, steadiness and support throughout the many years this work took shape, from primary school to adulthood. You all had a hand in shaping the man I became, and I will forever be grateful to have you as my brothers.

Some people helped by asking questions. Others helped by knowing when not to. Both forms mattered.

Duncan and Chris also foster. Watching care chosen and practised in the present, without performance or sentiment, has been a reminder of what commitment looks like when it is lived rather than spoken about.

Any errors, omissions or interpretations in this work remain my own.